THE MILITANT MINISTRY

THE KNUBEL-MILLER LECTURES FOR 1963

The Militant Ministry

People and Pastors

of the

Early Church and Today

by

Hans-Ruedi Weber

Board of Publication of the Lutheran Church in America
Philadelphia

CONTENTS

INTRODUCTION

In the Western world God's people settled down for centuries in the camps and institutions of the *corpus christianum*. During that period church structures and ministries developed which served their purpose well. Now, however, industrialization and the eroding power of secularization, the growth of militant ideologies and the forceful political, cultural and religious self-assertion of nations and continents beyond the old *corpus christianum* have brought about a new situation. Almost everywhere the church is becoming a minority in a world which does not stand in awe before the miracles of God but is fascinated by the miracles of technology. Once again God's people on earth must therefore set out from their safe camps, leave behind the fleshpots of Egypt and become God's pilgrim people on the way to the world of tomorrow. Once again Christians have to discern what patterns of ministry and structures of church life are now best suited for true worship, witness and service.

In this process of discernment very little can be done by books and lectures. Groups of Christians involved in the struggle of faith in the midst of this changing world will have to discover and shape new forms of ministry step by step. They may be helped, however, by the criteria of judgment which the biblical message gives and which were operative among the early Christians when they entered the bewildering new world of the Roman Empire. In fact those first four centuries of church history are for us today

more relevant than the Reformation history which happened within a still continuing *corpus christianum*. The
following lectures are, therefore, constructed in such a way
that in the introduction to each chapter one particular
aspect of the struggle of the militant church is set in its
early Christian environment; in the first part of each
chapter that aspect is then examined on the basis of the
writings of the New Testament and the experience of the
early church; and in the second part of each chapter some
implications are shown for the ministry of all baptized and
their ministers today. Throughout this book the term "ministry" refers to the calling and task of Christ and *all* members
of God's people (it is therefore often synonymous with the
ministry of the laity), while the term "ministers" is used in a
more restricted way, designating those church members who
have received a calling for a special office within and for
God's people, such as pastors, missionaries and bishops. The
five aspects of the church's struggle dealt with in the following chapters are: (1) *Baptism* as the initiation into the
ranks of the militant church and as the mark of true Christian life; (2) *the mission of peace* as the purpose of the
militant church which gives it its apostolic character; (3)
the equipment of grace given for service, which confers on
each baptized and the whole church a charismatic character;
(4) *the sacrificial way of life* and ministering which gives the
suffering of those involved in the battle of faith a peculiar
quality; and (5) *the true Christian joy* which reflects the
victory at Easter and is a foretaste of the kingdom.

While preparing the manuscript of these lectures I was
much involved in the drafting of the memorandum on
"Christ's ministry through his whole church and its ministers," which was sent by the Department on the Laity of the
World Council of Churches to the Fourth World Conference

on Faith and Order at Montreal, 1963 (published in *Laity,* No. 15, May 1963, pp. 13–39). There is, therefore, considerable overlapping with regard to content between these lectures and the above mentioned memorandum. Indeed, most of the insights contained in these lectures are the fruit of a long process of ecumenical study and conversation, initiated by the Department on the Laity. In the notes I have referred to literature which proved helpful to me in thinking about the subject of the ministry of the church and its ministers. It is impossible, however, to refer to each of the innumerable conversations which are at the root of so many of the following thoughts. To all those who during the last decade accompanied me on that exciting voyage of discovery with regard to the ministry of the laity and its implications for the militant church I want to express my thanks. Many of them will recognize in the following pages insights which came to us while together we were studying the Bible or speaking and praying about the present state of the church.

These lectures are written from a particular angle. Faced with the choice either to add another general book to the countless list of books and pamphlets on the ministry of the laity and the authority and function of ministers, or to examine one limited and as yet little explored aspect of this subject, I chose the latter. While rereading the New Testament and the studies about the early church I was impressed with the prominence of the military terminology: Christ as the victor over powers and principalities, as the victorious victim, and the church as the *militia Christi,* participating in Christ's struggle for cosmic peace. This military imagery has received little or no attention in the abundant modern literature about the ministry of the laity and the authority and function of ministers. Therefore I chose to emphasize particularly the military imagery of the

New Testament and the ancient church. Writing from such a limited standpoint one cannot claim to express the whole truth, but I trust that this partial truth will be corrected and complemented by others. Moreover, I hope that it may help some laymen and ministers to discern what their particular task is today in the battle of faith of the militant church.

Finally I would like to thank Miss Elizabeth Baker and Miss Renate Siebel for getting the manuscript ready for print. Above all, my thanks go to the Board of Theological Education of the Lutheran Church in America for the invitation to deliver these lectures as the Knubel-Miller Lectures—1963 in Philadelphia, Minneapolis, Chicago, Los Angeles, Nashville and Gettysburg. (The substance of this book was also used for a series of lectures and Bible studies at the World Consultation on Lay Training at the Ecumenical Institute, Château de Bossey, May, 1963). This invitation gave me not only the joy of visiting the United States once again, of coming to know and to love the Lutheran Church in America and of experiencing anew the most cordial American hospitality, but it became also the welcome occasion to dig more deeply in the treasure-land of the New Testament and to learn from the struggle of the early Christians.

H.-R. W.

Château de Bossey
May, 1963

AUTHOR'S NOTE

The New Testament quotations are taken from the New English Bible, unless indicated otherwise in the text or in the footnotes. Readers will soon discover that I am very much indebted to the monumental work initiated by Gerhard Kittel (ed.), *Theologisches Wörterbuch zum Neuen Testament* (Stuttgart, 1933——), which in the notes is abbreviated with *T.W.z.N.T.* Texts of Early Christian Fathers (I Clement, Ignatius, Apology of Justin) are quoted from *Library of Christian Classics,* Vol. I (London and Philadelphia, 1953). All other quotations are taken from the English publications indicated in the footnotes or have been translated by the author himself.

1

BAPTIZED TO JOIN A STRUGGLE

The event which illustrates best what these lectures are about must have happened early on an Easter morning. Even before cockcrow a group of people had gathered on that hilltop on the island of Rhodes in the Mediterranean where today the Orthodox monastery Philerimos stands. It happened some centuries after the apostle Paul had visited that beautiful island on his adventurous journey to Jerusalem.

They were simple people, for the most part probably slaves, and they gathered at a place for baptism: a big cross lying flat, cut in the rock of the hilltop, some eight feet long and six feet wide and three feet deep, with a step going from the west down into the cross, which was then filled with water, and a step going up towards the east, in the direction of the rising sun where today you can still see the ruins of a very old chapel.[1]

This handful of people of Rhodes had come to know Christ. The message of an evangelist or more likely the strange quality of life of the Christians who lived among them had caught their attention. They had been received as catechumens and had learned from their teacher the mighty acts of God. In the week before Easter they were introduced to the mysteries of faith. They were taught the Creed and the Ten Commandments, and in fasting and prayer they had prepared themselves for the decisive event of baptism. Now they had gathered at that baptistry which

1

reminded them of the cross of Christ. Each one turned to
the dark west and cried into this darkness: "I renounce you,
Satan, and all your service and all your works!" Let us not
forget that Satan for them was not just a figure of speech
but a frightening reality with great power, accusing every
man, inflicting illness and plagues on the whole creation.
For many centuries western Christians have tended to dis-
regard what the New Testament tells about "powers and
principalities." Individual man is free in his own man-made
world, and each can decide as he wishes—so many thought
until the recent earthquakes in world history taught us
better. We know now how fear or an ideology can take hold
of whole nations like a fever, how an evil group spirit can
carry the masses away and cause them to do things which no
individual would do of his own free will. Modern psychiatry
and group psychology confirm what we all know from experience, and modern sociology explains how each of us is ines-
capably caught up in social structures and images of our
time to which we conform. Hidden persuaders tyrannize us
in the East and the West. It is therefore not astonishing that
in recent years biblical scholarship has again turned its
attention to the texts about the powers and principalities.[2]

Indeed, the powers and principalities have lost none of
their reality, although we now understand them differently
from the New Testament writers and although we cannot
so easily visualize them as those converts of Rhodes did on
that Easter morning when they challenged Satan by publicly
deserting him. Some of these men and women must have
trembled when making this act of rebellion. Yet they knew
what they did. Their teachers had told them how Christ had
fought against these powers and principalities and how he
had won the victory over them. At about that time those
famous pictures of *Christus militans* were painted showing

Christ as the triumphant victor—standing with one foot on the head of the dragon and the other on the head of a lion—and the sign of his struggle and victory, the cross.[3] This must have been the image of Christ[4] in the minds of the converts of Rhodes when they renounced the devil and subsequently were anointed with the oil of exorcism.

After this first act in their baptism, which to them was the sign and seal of their conversion, each convert stepped into the cross. Three times he was in a dramatic way buried in the water of the cross-baptistry. A presbyter asked: "Do you believe in God the Father Almighty?" "I believe," said the convert; and to show that belief is not just an intellectual thing but something which threatens the whole of our old life as lived until that moment, the convert was totally immersed in the water. "Do you believe in Christ Jesus, the Son of God . . .?" "I believe," and again the one making the confession was buried in the water, becoming one with the cross and the Crucified. "Do you believe in the Holy Spirit, in the Holy Church, and the resurrection of the flesh?" "I believe," said each convert and was immersed for the third time. The teaching of the apostle Paul about baptism must have been tremendously meaningful for these early converts of Rhodes. Probably never during their life did they forget that in their baptism they were baptized into the death of Christ. To say it in Paul's own words: "By baptism we were buried with him, and lay dead, in order that, as Christ was raised from the dead in the splendour of the Father, so also we might set our feet upon the new path of life. . . . We know that the man we once were has been crucified with Christ, for the destruction of the sinful self, so that we may no longer be the slaves of sin. . . . But if we thus died with Christ, we believe that we shall also come to life with him" (Rom. 6:4–8). So, in the second act of their baptism the converts of Rhodes were taken into the death and life of Christ, into his struggle and victory. From now on they were no more to be puppets for powers and principalities to play with—just as we are not meant to be puppets for the hidden persuaders of propaganda, advertisements, ideologies and all the pressures to conform. From now on they and all who are baptized are incorporated into Christ's army, into the *militia Christi,* for the struggle of faith.

Therefore a third act followed immediately in the oldest baptismal liturgy known to us, which is at the basis of this description[5] and which may very well have been used for that baptism at Rhodes: stepping out of the cross, the newly baptized were anointed with the oil of thanksgiving. They put on their clothes and were led into the church building where the congregation was gathered. There the act of chrismation took place. The bishop laid his hand on the converts and prayed the following significant prayer: "O Lord God, who didst count these Thy servants worthy of deserving the forgiveness of sins by the laver of regeneration, make them worthy to be filled with Thy Holy Spirit and send upon them Thy grace, that they may serve Thee according to Thy will. . . ." Then the bishop anointed them and thus they were fully taken into God's people. The kiss of peace was exchanged as a symbol of this and the baptism service ended with the celebration of the eucharist, the feast of victory at the cross.

I.

While describing this baptismal service I have begun to use military terms. This is no accident. Paul himself did so, when he continued his already quoted teaching about baptism with the following words: "You must no longer put the members of your body at sin's disposal, as weapons[6] for doing wrong. No: put yourselves at the disposal of God, as dead men raised to life; yield your bodies to him as weapons for doing right; for sin shall no longer be your master, because you are no longer under law, but under the grace of God" (Rom. 6:13–14). "Let us therefore throw off the deeds of darkness and put on our armour as soldiers of the light" (Rom. 13:12). Christ had already occasionally used military language,[7] but it was the apostle Paul who introduced many military terms into the Christian vocabulary and who began to describe the whole life of the church as a participation in Christ's struggle with the powers and principalities. Especially his own missionary work, and that of his fellow ministers, Paul considered as a continuous battle. Also later New Testament letters which were written under the influence of Paul are full of this military terminology.[8] It is therefore no wonder that the Christian tradition pictures the apostle Paul with a sword in his hand, according to the advice he gave to the Christians of his time: "For sword, take that which the Spirit gives you—the words that come from God" (Eph. 6:17).

The early church continued to see its life and mission as a military service under Christ the Imperator, as Adolf Harnack has shown in a most interesting study on the *militia Christi*.[9]

In the oldest Christian document outside the New Testament writings, a letter which in the name of the church in Rome is addressed by the presbyter Clement to the church in Corinth (A.D. 96/97), the following revealing passage occurs: "Let us realize how near he [i.e., God] is, and that none of our thoughts or of the ideas we have escapes his notice. It is right, therefore, that we should not be deserters, dis-

obeying his will" (21:3—4). In the early church infidelity to
God was called desertion while in Old Testament times it
was usually called adultery.

This hangs together with the old Christian concept of
baptism. When at the beginning of the second century Ignatius, the bishop of Antioch, was led by a military guard to his
martyrdom in Rome, he wrote to his colleague, the bishop
Polycarp in Smyrna: "Let none of you prove a deserter. Let
your baptism be your arms!" (6:2). Indeed, baptism was
soon considered as the soldier's oath at the entry to the
militant church. When in the middle of the second century,
Justin, a Christian teacher in Rome, addressed his defence
of the Christian faith to the Roman Emperor, the august
Senate and the whole Roman people, he compared the
loyalty which Christians have sworn to Christ with the oath
of the soldiers in the Roman army (1:39). Soon the technical
term for the military oath, the Latin word *sacramentum,*
was taken over by the church in order to designate baptism.
In the writings of Origen, the great teacher of the theological
school in Alexandria at the beginning of the third century,
the term *sacramentum militiae* is used several times in connection with baptism. Origen began to call all Christians
"soldiers of Christ" (*milites Christi*) and he spoke about the
church as "the military camp of the Lord" (*castra Domini*).

However, it was the son of an officer in the Roman garrison
at Carthage, Tertullian, a contemporary of Origen, who
firmly rooted the *militia Christi* terminology in the Christian
vocabulary. He for the first time called Christ the *imperator.*
In the midst of severe persecutions he wrote to potential
martyrs: "We have already been called to the status of
soldiers of the living God when we spoke [at our baptism]
the words of the military oath," the *sacramentum* (*Ep. ad
Mart.* 3). "On the basis of this *sacramentum* I am a soldier

and am being challenged by the enemies . . .; defending my oath I fight, am wounded, knocked down and killed. This destiny has been assigned to the soldier by the one who has taken him for duty by such a *sacramentum*" (*Scorp.* 4). This was not just a way of expressing himself, but a reality. Adolf Harnack who knew the early church better than any other modern scholar wrote: "Tertullian and with him the Latin Christians knew themselves in a real and literal way to be soldiers of Christ. At baptism they swore to him the military oath, they promised themselves to Christ, they now belong to him and as his soldiers are responsible to him only." "In the centuries after Tertullian the sermons and exhortations in the Western Latin Church abound with military images of the soldier's service, of military discipline and of the fight. Indeed, one can say that this scheme and these images were those most often used" for designating the church and its work.[10]

A most revealing indication as to the strength of this Christian consciousness of being the militant church is the change of meaning in the Latin word *paganus* in the fourth and fifth centuries. The term (which is of course at the root of the English word "pagan") originally meant, especially in the western part of the Roman Empire, "the civilian" as opposed to "the soldier." Tertullian, however, had already written that each Christian, including the civilian (the *paganus*), is a soldier (namely of Christ) and each soldier of the Roman Emperor is in God's eyes a civilian (a *paganus*). In the Latin church Christians only were considered to be *milites* in the real sense of this term and all the non-Christians were therefore considered as "civilians," i.e., as *pagani*, as "pagans."[11] Another Latin term, *statio*, which means a "position," e.g., the place of anchorage, and which originally had little to do with military language, became a technical

military term through the fact that the church used it to
describe the battle position of the militant church.[12]

This conception of the *militia Christi* and of baptism as
the initiation into the militant church can throw a new
light on the much debated questions about the role of lay
people and of the especially ordained ministers of the
church. But before showing some of the implications for
today it is necessary to point to at least two inherent dangers
in using military language for speaking about the church,
its members and ministers. Indeed, the military terminology
soon strengthened some developments in the early church
which we have come to see as very dangerous or even wrong
developments, departing from the biblical message.

This had already begun in the letter of Clement quoted
earlier. He wrote: "Really in earnest, then, brothers, we
must march under his [i. e., Christ's] irreproachable orders.
Let us note with what discipline, readiness and obedience
those who serve under our [i.e., the Roman] generals carry
out orders. Not everybody is a general, colonel, captain,
sergeant, and so on. But each in his own rank carries out the
orders of the emperor and of the generals" (37:1–3). It is
symptomatic that the man who wrote this is known in the
Roman bishop lists as the second or third bishop of Rome,
thus as one of the successors of Peter. Instead of illustrating
the biblical message, the military image began to add to and
alter the original content. A whole hierarchy of generals,
colonels, captains, etc., was placed in between Christ the
emperor and the ordinary soldiers. Among the soldiers of
Christ there was now a small group who gave orders and a
large group who had simply to obey. "The military analogy
favours the clergy: of course, all Christians are soldiers; but
just because of that they have to obey their leaders, the

presbyters!"[13] The apostles Paul would certainly never have
spoken in this way, although he too had much to say about
authority, obedience and different tasks within the militant
church.[14]

Another dangerous development fostered by the military
terminology becomes clear in the writings of Origen. In
his time both the ordinary lay membership of the church
and what was then called the clergy had lost much of the
fervor of the first and second generation Christians. Many
were world-conformed. Could these really be called soldiers
of Christ? Origen must have meditated much on the text in
II Timothy 2:4 which says: "A soldier on active service will
not let himself be involved in civilian affairs; he must be
wholly at his commanding officer's disposal." This military
analogy was taken too literally and turned around. Origen
said now: Those who do not involve themselves in civilian
affairs are the real soldiers, thus the ascetics. So Origen became the father of the concept that the ascetics and later
the monks and nuns are the real soldiers of Christ. They
fight in the place of and for the sake of the ordinary laity.
Harnack made the following comment about this exegesis of
II Timothy 2:4: "This principle which is laid down here
for the first time and which is proved with a military
analogy has later led to an extraordinarily rich development:
*it has not created the state of the clergy as distinct from the
state of the laity, but it has given it the strongest support.*
It has had a decisive influence on the developing conception
of the monastic life. It is one of those tremendous maxims
whose implementation has impregnated the whole society
and changed its character. In all centuries these words stand
above the Catholic sacerdos and Catholic monastic life. 'No
soldier let himself be involved in civilian affairs.' Too often
these words have become a declaration of war; above all

they have led later to a devaluation of civilian life and of the civilian vocation."[15] Indeed, it is a tragic irony of history that in the same centuries when the impact of Christian baptism changed the meaning of the word *paganus,* within the church itself baptism was devaluated. The unity of God's people was lost. A great gulf grew between the "real Christians" (i.e., ascetics) and plenipotentiary representatives of Christ (i.e., the hierarchy) on the one side and the mass of immature ordinary Christians (i.e., the laity) on the other. In itself the development of a differentiation within the militant church is according to God's will and has its origins already in the New Testament. Neither the establishment of a group of clergy nor the growth of monasticism *within* the corporate life of the church need necessarily devaluate the ministry of the laity. On the contrary: both can help the laity to grow into maturity. But a wrong use of the military terminology has led to the separation of priests and monks from the laity. Priests and monks became the accepted Christian type, the image of a true Christian. They began to set the patterns of church life and holiness, and in their hands all authority was laid. Instead of being the *militia Christi* on the march, the church thus became a bulwark for half-committed civilians with a staff of professional officers and some troops of mercenaries.

II.

After this glimpse of what baptism meant to the early Christians and how they came to consider themselves as the militant church, it is possible to draw some first conclusions for the life and work of church members and their ministers today.

1. The first thing we must insist upon when we speak about the laity is *conversion*. Some one hundred years ago a book was written on "the dangers of an unconverted clergy." This danger is still quite acute, but now it is more than time that a book be written about "the dangers of an unconverted laity."[16] Lay movements, as well as talks, articles and books about the laity, are quite popular nowadays,[17] but such movements and talks are dangerous for the true life and mission of the church if they do not lead to a new reflection and insistence on conversion. Otherwise lay movements inevitably become pressure groups within the church or, what is worse, make the church itself a pressure group within society. This leads to the worst kind of clericalization, namely, the lording of the church over the world.

Only a converted laity is fit to fight according to the mind of Christ. Yet, what does this mean: "A converted laity"? For a long time many Christians and theologians have shied away from using the term "conversion," because it is used so onesidedly by an aggressive wing of Christianity which also likes to use military terms such as "evangelism campaigns" or "missionary strategy." Conversion is there thought of mainly in individualistic terms, as an act of man or rather of his soul. Evangelism campaigns then look rather like a sort of raid by American Indians who invade the enemy territory, collect scalps and quickly retreat to their safe strongholds. What is brought back from such campaigns is indeed often scalps only, namely the scalps of some religious emotions, while the whole man—with his body and intellect, his essential ties with a multitude of small and large groups in society, his responsibilities in the family, in industry and commerce, and the world of political affairs—is left behind unconverted.

When the Bible speaks about conversion, it does so always in the context of what God has accomplished for us. Like a mighty eagle he has rescued Israel out of its bondage in Egypt and brought it to himself (Ex. 19:4). He has forcefully torn us out of the domain of darkness and brought us away into the kingdom of his Son (Col. 1:13). The verbs which describe God's saving and converting act often remind us of the battle between Christ and the powers of darkness.[18] It is on the basis of this continuing struggle in which the decisive victory has already been won that God calls us to conversion: "Be no more slaves, puppets and collaborators of the powers and principalities, but having been rescued from their domination, become fellow-soldiers in the militant church." In this call to conversion total man with all his links with society is mobilized. This is the true intention of the passage in II Timothy 2:3–4 discussed earlier about the soldier on active service and entirely at the disposal of Christ, his commanding officer. This call must not be mistaken for a call to otherworldliness, but to a new stand in and for the world. The biblical terms for conversion mean indeed not an exodus, an escape, but a change of direction by which we gain new criteria of judgment and a new purpose in life. It is never just a negative conversion from something, but always also a positive conversion for some new task towards a new aim in fellowship with Christ.[19] After conversion, therefore, nobody must stand still and remain entranced with his conversion experience. For he has joined an army on the march. It then becomes clear that conversion is not only the primary and basic "yes" of a man to Christ in answer to God's gracious "yes" to his world. It is also a lifelong and often hidden process which happens in the sequence of obedient responses to the demands of Christ in the decisions of everyday life and work in order

not to become a deserter. Without this conversion there are
no laymen worthy of the name.

The early church knew this, and the converts of Rhodes
were forcefully reminded of it when they had to renounce
publicly the devil, his service and all his works. This was
no cheap baptism. In certain cases the converts had to
change their jobs if these were felt to be in contradiction
to active service as soldiers of Christ. Unless we recover
this intimate connection between conversion and baptism—
or as Paul usually puts it, between faith and baptism[20]—all
our talk about the ministry of the laity in the militant church
will remain shallow and irrelevant. This is not necessarily
a call for the establishment of believers' baptism in all
churches. On the basis of the New Testament it can neither
be proved that children were actually baptized nor that
only adults were baptized. In the missionary situation of
those days believers' baptism was probably the norm and
infant baptism the exception. Yet very early in church history children of parents joining the church and children
of Christian parents were baptized and the faith of the
parents and the local church was then considered as initially
standing for the faith of the baptized children.[21] In the
Orthodox church where, generally, infant baptism is administered, the creed is spoken by the godparents even in the
case of the baptism of adults, showing thus that not just
the belief of the individual Christian is related to his baptism but the belief of the total church. However, there
seems to be a growing trend to re-establish believers' baptism
as the norm with the baptism of the children of believing
parents as the exception, especially in areas of former majority churches, where the preaching of cheap grace has
led to the administration of cheap baptisms (and vice versa)
and where the church finds itself now suddenly in a new

missionary situation.[22] In the ecumenical search for truth the question of believers' versus infant baptism still remains open. There is no doubt, however, that under no circumstances may belief be lacking when baptism is administered.[23] This inevitably means that church discipline will have to be re-established so that the church may dare to make a provisional decision about who belongs to the militant church and who has never joined the battle of faith or who is in process of becoming a deserter.[24] In the Lutheran church in New Guinea infant baptism is withheld if the faith of the parents or of the local congregation is obviously lacking.[25]

2. Having first seen the conversion aspect of baptism we must secondly insist on the *incorporation* aspect. Not only is it impossible to stand still after baptism but it is also impossible to remain alone. We do not become solitary freelance soldiers but we join the marching company of God. This aspect has been preserved in most baptism liturgies. We are baptized into the common life of the body of Christ. We are now in the fellowship with him and with other fellow-soldiers.[26] In the early church the service of baptism therefore led up to the celebration of the eucharist. In our time, however, the church is deeply divided at the Lord's Table although it has found a far-reaching consensus with regard to baptism. To recognize one another's baptism while remaining divided at the Lord's Table is a dangerous anomaly. It continuously devaluates baptism and makes the feast of unity a constant demonstration of division.

Equally serious is the division of the baptized in the midst of the battle of faith in the life of families, work communities and neighborhoods, in the life of a nation and the living together of various races, classes and nations. Denominational differences become quite irrelevant when we are faced with decisions about the right education of youth, the responsible management of labor, or the technical assistance programs to underfed nations. Here at least, at the front of the battle of faith, one would expect unity among all those who through the *sacramentum* of baptism have become members of the militant church. In fact many laymen have found at such frontiers of decision a unity which reaches far beyond the limits of their particular denominations. But all of us have also made the staggering discovery that at the frontier of decision Christian unity often breaks down. This may be an indication that we are still slaves of the powers and principalities of our age, puppets of propaganda and social prejudice with pagan criteria of judgment which in a subtle way have been imposed upon us. In this case we are still unconverted laity and must do everything to smash our pagan criteria of judgment and to grow into the mind of Christ. Different or opposing decisions by we who have received the one baptism may also spring from basic differences in our attitude towards the Bible, our understanding of the biblical message and of Christian faith. In this case our task is to search together for the full truth, sharing the partial truths each of us has received, and correcting one another in the partial heresies to which each of us succumbs. Yet it may also be that divergent decisions stem from our obedient response to different callings, each one in his own particular situation and according to the particular gifts of grace he has received. In such a case we must not impose uniformity, but rejoice in our diversity. We obey a living Lord and not a once-for-all, fixed set of so-called "Christian principles." The incorporation through the one baptism does not lead to uniformity and Christian conformism, but to a constant response to the orders of Christ who

alone knows fully God's strategy. One member can check
and help the other in this process of reaching an obedient
choice. Sometimes a whole troop of Christians reaches a corporate decision and is called to corporate action. More often
each must stand alone in his particular place at the front.
And there are also those moments when we do not know,
when we err in no-man's-land and are not certain whether
we still fight with Christ's army or have already become
deserters. Then we may remember that Christ remains in
communion with us and is not only the commanding officer
but also the good shepherd who seeks those who are lost.

3. Baptism has a third, most important aspect, one which
in many churches today is either forgotten or appears only
in a devaluated form in the act of confirmation. After having
renounced the devil and having been incorporated into the
cross of Christ, the converts of Rhodes were chrismated,
which means nothing else than ordained. Indeed, baptism
is also the *ordination* into the laity. It is the basic ordination
of each Christian, his commissioning to join the struggle of
faith.[27] In the confirmation liturgy of the Church of South
India, which is considered an integral part of the total rite
of baptism, those who are confirmed are asked the following
question: "Do you acknowledge yourselves bound to confess
the faith of Christ crucified and risen, to fight manfully
under his banner, and to continue his faithful soldiers and
servants unto your lives' end, bearing witness to him both in
word and in deed?" Later in the service the minister, and
sometimes the whole congregation, prays that God may
send down the Holy Spirit upon those who are confirmed.[28]
This prayer is similar to the Epiklesis, the eucharistic prayer
in which the minister asks for the coming of the Spirit to

the elements of bread and wine so that in them Christ may really be present among us. In the same way the church prays that the Spirit may descend on the baptized, through his power change them from *pagani* into *milites,* from civilians into soldiers, and ordain them for joining Christ's struggle, suffering and victory. As a sign and seal of this ordination through the Holy Spirit the minister lays his hand on each one baptized.

The aspect of commissioning stands at the center of the ceremony which sometimes replaces, or at least complements, baptism in that Christian movement of today which uses military terminology most extensively, the Salvation Army. This ceremony is called "The enrolment as soldier." All who desire to become full members of the Salvation Army must read, accept and sign the "Articles of War" which contain the Articles of Doctrine of the Salvation Army and a number of promises (for instance, the promise to support the "Salvation War" as far as possible, to obey the lawful orders of their officers and at all times to live as soldiers of Christ and of the Salvation Army). They are then received by an officer under the Salvation Army flag with the words: "In the name of the General, I accept your declaration and greet you as soldiers of the Salvation Army and comrades serving under the flag of blood and fire. . . ."[29] We may be shocked by this language and rightly feel that here the military image reaches the absurb. It would also be easy to show great dangers and shortcomings in such a commissioning, for instance the onesided emphasis on man's individual decision. Nevertheless, we need to take seriously also this manifestation of Christ's church today. First of all because of the Salvation Army's exemplary devotion to witness and service in the toughest spots of our society, but also because this reminds

us of the fact that in baptism each member of the church
has been ordained for a total devotion to witness and service
in the world.

A layman is indeed not somebody who has *not* studied
theology, who is *not* in full-time Christian service or who is
not ordained. Who would like to be labelled such an "is
not"? One cannot define the laity in this negative way. The
total event of baptism confers something: it confers the state
of grace, a ministry and spiritual authority. Laymen have,
for instance, authority in theology. The knowledge of God's
person and work which men and women gain as they seek
to be obedient to his will in concrete secular situations is
not less important than the technical knowledge of the
Bible, of doctrine and church history which ministers and
professional theologians acquire. Theologically illiterate laymen can be just as dangerous as theologically illiterate ministers. Churches should therefore spend at least as much
money and man-power for the theological education of the
laity as they do now for the theological education of ministers. Laymen in the biblical sense of this word are also not
just people who in their spare time go to church or do some
voluntary church work. They *are* the church, the *laos*, i.e.,
members of God's People,[30] and they serve God full-time
through their secular jobs. Finally, laymen are certainly not
unordained. They have received the basic ordination of baptism, they are "chrismated Christians," as our Orthodox
brethren say.[31]

4. This insistence on the basic ordination of baptism
which each Christian receives raises immediately the question
about the role of *special ordinations* in the church. If the
ministry of the church is the same as the ministry of the laity
—and in these lectures the two expressions are indeed used

interchangeably—what remains then for especially ordained ministers? How is their service to be related to the serving laity? This question will be one of the topics in all the following chapters. Here I simply want to state that the rediscovery of the ministry of the laity indeed challenges traditional conceptions about the authority and function of especially ordained ministers. These ministers are baptized, and the basic, once-for-all and life-long ordination of baptism remains valid for them. Every minister is therefore first of all an ordinary soldier in the company of God under the orders of Christ who alone is the commanding officer. For this reason it is wrong to define the ministers over against the laity or vice versa.

However, the basic ordination of baptism does not exclude subsequent ordinations for a special task. The militant church needs soldiers who are set apart for[32] the work of pioneering, for services of communications between the commanding officer and the fighting army and between the different units of this army. Some must be set apart for training and for oversight. All these functions just mentioned are fulfilled by the ministers of the church. And let us not forget that humble but very important service which each pastor is called to fulfil, the service of the army cook who provides food for the fighting army.

2

SENT ON A MISSION OF PEACE

In spring 1947 an Arab shepherd was looking for a goat that had got lost. It was in the wild valley of Wadi Qumrân, which falls away from the wilderness of Judea to the Dead Sea in Palestine. Being weary he sat down and amused himself by throwing stones into a hole in the cliff in front of him. Suddenly he heard something breaking inside the hole. Frightened he ran away, but the next day he came back with his cousin and together they explored the narrow cavern. They found little that interested them, only some jars and in one of them three scrolls with an old script which they could not decipher. However, when about a year later these scrolls, and other manuscripts which had meanwhile been found, came into the hands of Jewish and Christian scholars in Jerusalem, more than interest was awakened. The "fever of Qumrân" began all over the world among Jewish and Christian scholars.[1] Many of these "Dead Sea Scrolls," as the newly discovered old manuscripts were called, proved to be portions of Old Testament books and of the Apocrypha. Yet among the scrolls there are also a few which give us most interesting information about the life of a Jewish sect of priestly origin, the Essenes, who had retreated from Jerusalem into the wilderness of Judea. They built a sort of monastery at Qumrân and lived there from the end of the second century B.C. until the first Jewish revolt when, in A.D. 68, the settlement of Qumrân was destroyed.

One of these scrolls of the Essenes—it actually was one of the first three found by the Arab shepherd—is called "The Rule for the War," or by the better known title given to it by its first editor: "The War of the Sons of Light against the Sons of Darkness."[2] Scholars still dispute the origin of this scroll, but it is quite possible that the document was written during the last phase of the settlement of the Essenes at Qumrân after the death of Herod the Great in 4 B.C., thus during the time of the earthly life of our Lord.[3] At that time the younger recruits of the community of Qumrân were as much filled with anti-Roman feelings as with religious fervor. The Rule for the War shows this attitude very clearly. A priest of Qumrân must have got hold of a military manual of Herod's army, because there are striking parallels in organization between Herod's military forces and the apocalyptic army of the sons of light. This military manual was then rewritten to become a description of the holy war against the sons of darkness. It is a war of extermination which lasts for exactly forty years. Each seventh year is a year of sabbath during which the war is at a complete standstill. The sons of light "exiled in the Desert of the Nations" (i.e., those coming from the Jewish diaspora) are to join forces with the sons of light who are "exiled in the Desert" (i.e., the Essenes at Qumrân). Together they will fight the war at the end of time in the "Desert of Jerusalem." In an almost mechanical way the army of the sons of light will go from victory to victory under the leadership of the priests and of two messianic figures, the High Priest and the Prince of the Congregation. This Rule for the War of the Essenes must have been an excellent piece of war propaganda for the Jewish nationalists in their preparation for the first Jewish revolt against Roman colonial power. It is quite possible that when the explosion of this first Jewish revolt

came, part of the community of Qumrân marched to Jerusalem after having hidden their manuscripts away in caves.
Yet this holy war was a pitiful failure.

During this same period the militant church was growing
in Jerusalem and Judea, in Antioch and from there onwards
towards the center of the Roman Empire, knowing that this
was only the first stage on its march towards the ends of the
whole inhabited world. Why has this handful of Christians
survived and grown into the world-wide church, while that
other group, the community of the Essenes of Qumrân, died
and was practically unknown until the discovery of the
Dead Sea Scrolls? Both knew themselves to be the army of
God. Both used sometimes strikingly similar language. Indeed it is quite possible that direct or indirect relationships
existed between the community of Qumrân and the early
church. Yet their whole outlook, nature and purpose were
quite different. A comparison between the Rule for the War
of Qumrân and the New Testament concept of the militant
church can teach us much about our own struggle of faith
in the world of today.[4]

I.

The following four differences between the community
of the War Scroll and the militant church are most striking
and illuminate the specific character of the latter. (1) Both
used military imagery, but the one became militarist while
the other remained (at least in theory) for centuries pacifist.
(2) Both were involved in a struggle, but the one struggled
to exterminate, while the other struggled for peace. (3) Both
aimed at victory; but the apparent victories of the one led
to defeat, while the other becomes the victim and as such
gains ultimate victory. (4) While the priests had absolute

authority in the one, each member is expected to be a responsible soldier in the other.

1. Both the text from Qumrân and the New Testament use military images. When the writer of the Rule for the War referred to weapons, war, hatred and extermination of enemies, he meant this literally. The members of the community of that Scroll must have rejoiced when the sign for the first Jewish revolt against the Roman colonial army was given. They were militarists in the deepest sense of the word. They looked forward eagerly to the "holy war," to "the day which He [God] appointed of old for the final battle against the Sons of Darkness" (1QM i:10). In this they continued a line which has its origin in the Old Testament and reached its climax in the books of Maccabees.[5]

For Christ also, as well as for his disciples and the early church, the military terminology was not just a figure of speech but a hard reality. Yet the military language never led them to military actions. When a disciple wanted to defend the Lord at his capture in the garden of Gethsemane, Jesus commanded: "Put up your sword. All who take the sword die by the sword. Do you suppose that I cannot appeal to my Father who would at once send to my aid more than twelve legions of angels?" (Matt. 26:52f.). Another time when Jesus wanted to prepare his disciples for the coming crisis, he said: "Whoever . . . has no sword, let him sell his cloak to buy one." But when he was misunderstood by the disciples, who took his words literally and said that there were two swords available, our Lord cut off the conversation with an almost ironic, "Enough, enough!" (Luke 22:36f.; cf. John 18:36). The New Testament and the early church broke with the tradition of holy wars. While using military terminology the early church was, at least in theory, strictly pacifist. Typical of their attitude is the episode when in Alexandria Saint Sabas was asked by his parents to become the military chaplain in the company which was under the command of his father. He answered, "I am a soldier in the company of God and I cannot abandon his army. Those who want to press me into desertion I can no longer call my parents."[6] This was also the firm conviction of that other son of an officer, Tertullian, who wrote, "Do you think it is permissible to make a military oath [*sacramentum*] to men after we have taken the divine oath [at baptism] and thus make an oath to another lord than Christ!" (*De Corona II*). In the centuries before Constantine Christians never resorted to the sword in order to preserve the life of the church or to foster its mission. Even in the midst of severe persecutions, and in provinces where the number of Christians was such as to guarantee a successful revolt, the call for a holy war did not ring out. In this we see the first great difference between the Rule for the War of Qumrân and the militant church. As a matter of fact, in the New Testament the terms "war" (*polemos*) and "quarrel" (*machē*) never describe the battle of faith. In some Old Testament books both of these terms were still used in a positive way for pointing to the mission of Israel, while in the whole New Testament they have a negative connotation. "The servant of the Lord must not be quarrelsome, but kindly towards all" (II Tim. 2:24).[7]

The mission of the militant church is therefore never a *polemos,* it is never "polemical." Of course church history shows us the contrary. There have been endless quarrels between churches and between the church and the world. If one cut out all polemical passages from theological literature, whole libraries would be reduced to nothing. Yet, we are not made soldiers of the militant church in order to fight one another or in order to quarrel with people of other faiths or no faith. There are no holy wars. All Christian crusades against non-Christians, whether the crusades against the Moslems in the Middle Ages or the crusades against the Communists in the twentieth century, are black spots in the history of the church. Of course Christians stand in the world and in the midst of its power politics. They are caught up in wars and will then have to decide what Christian obedience means in the war situation. This has indeed been one of the most divisive issues among Christians. Already in the first centuries there were Christians who despite the theoretical pacifism of the church remained soldiers in the Roman army.[8] Actually, it was in and through the army that the breakthrough from the pagan and anti-Christian Roman Empire to the Christian state of Constantine and Theodosius took place.[9] Since then among Christians there have always been pacifists and those who joined earthly armies. Whatever our own decision of obedience in this grave question may be, the following two things are quite clear: the church may never be among the warmongers, but it must on the contrary support all honest movements for peace, not only the Christian ones. On the other hand, Christian pacifists should never take themselves too seriously, as though their action were in some way special, for it belongs to the very heart of the mission of the total church to fight and suffer for peace.

2. This reveals a second great difference between the sons of light of Qumrân and the sons of light who have been enlightened by Christ. The Rule for the War speaks of a struggle to exterminate. The trumpets of persecution used by that army bear the revealing inscription: "God has smitten all the children of Darkness. He will not turn back His anger

until He has consumed them" (1QM iii:9). Theirs is a mission of hatred, of war in which by the power of God's hand
the enemies' "corpses have been flung forth, with none to
bury them" (1QM xi:1).

The militant church, however, is sent on a mission of
peace. It has received the news of Christ's victory in order
to become ambassadors of this "good news of peace through
Jesus Christ, who is Lord of all," as Peter once put it to Cor-
nelius (Acts 10:36). According to the testimony of John, our
Lord himself gave the apostles peace as his parting gift (John
14:27) and connected it with his victory at the cross. "I have
told you all this so that in me you may find peace. In the
world you will have trouble. But courage! The victory is
mine; I have conquered the world" (John 16:33). However,
this parting gift of peace is no summons to sleep, but a
trumpet call to break up and go as ambassadors of peace to
the end of the earth and till the ends of time. We see the
apostles going from town to town, entering the houses and
obeying the Lord who said: "Wish the house peace as you
enter it, so that, if it is worthy, your peace may descend on
it" (Matt. 10:12f.). How far we are here from that other
document of the same period, the mission of hatred in the
Rule for the War! Neither the sons of light of Qumrân nor
the sons of the militant church have a peaceful life. Both
have to hasten to the fight. The fanatics of the War Scroll
pursue their enemies in order to kill them. All "shall pursue
the enemy to annihilate him in the battle of God unto his
eternal extinction" (1QM ix:5). The soldiers of the militant
church, however, have to pursue peace (Rom. 14:19; II Tim.
2:22; Heb. 12:14; I Pet. 3:11). In the famous passage in the
letter to the Ephesians about the armor of a Christian, peace
is connected with the putting on of boots, with going forth.
Several times peace is actually called a way (Luke 1:39;

19:42; Rom. 3:17). On this highroad of peace blood flows, yet not the blood of enemies as is the case according to the Rule for the War (1QM ix:8–9), but the blood of Christ. "Through him God chose to reconcile the whole universe to himself, making peace through the shedding of his blood upon the cross" (Col. 1:20). This was no cheap peace, and those who are sent on the mission for peace have to pay something of the cost of it. Paul spoke much about this in his epistles to the Corinthians: "From first to last this has been the work of God. He has reconciled us men to himself through Christ, and he has enlisted us in this service of reconciliation. What I mean is, that God was in Christ reconciling the world to himself, no longer holding men's misdeeds against them, and that he has entrusted us with the message of reconciliation. We come therefore as Christ's ambassadors" (II Cor. 5:18–20). In this connection Paul gave a whole list of things which are implied in this ambassadorship: "Like men condemned to death in the arena," "a spectacle to the whole universe," "fools for Christ's sake," "hungry, thirsty and in rags," "hard-pressed on every side," "bewildered," "hunted," "struck down," "flogged," "imprisoned," "mobbed," "overworked," "sleepless," "starving," etc. (I Cor. 3:18–4:13; II Cor. 4:1–15; 5:14–6:10). This is the Pauline picture of the ambassadors of Christ, of the pioneers in the militant church.

If today we want to remain in this succession we may not look for a soothing "peace of mind." We may not worship the idol of success. It is not for nothing that our Lord once warned us, saying paradoxically, "You must not think that I have come to bring peace to the earth; I come not to bring peace, but a sword" (Matt. 10:34). The mission of peace is a struggle which may cost more than our peace of mind or our promotion—it may cost our life.

3. This points to a third important difference between
the text from Qumrân and the Bible. According to the
Rule for the War the sons of light go from victory to victory. Their conquests are almost mechanical, and even the
years of sabbath when no fighting is allowed apparently
do not set back their march to victory (1QM ii:8f.).[10] The
soldiers of the War Scroll have their eyes fixed firmly on
the coming day of final war and triumph. They are ex-
tremely self-confident and know exactly who belongs to
God's army and who has to be destroyed. Their own casual-
ties are only once slightly hinted at (1QM xvi:11).

Quite contrary to this, victory seems to be against the
militant church. The front is never quite clear. Some of
those who seem to be fellow-soldiers, like Judas Iscariot,
suddenly become enemies; many others who were the most
bitter enemies, like Paul, become pioneers of the militant
church. The battle is not only against the powers and principalities facing the church, but also against their infiltra-
tion in the midst of the ranks of Christ's army. The letters
to the seven churches at the beginning of the book of Revelation are especially revealing in this matter (Rev. 2–3). The
language of this last book of the Bible sounds strange to
modern ears but, whatever we think about it, its main message has been relevant to the militant church all through
the centuries. Here it is in the barest outline.[11]

The victory has been won. The motion picture of the
book of Revelation begins therefore with the appearance of
Christus Victor who says, "Do not be afraid. I am the first
and the last, and I am the living one; for I was dead and
now I am alive for evermore, and I hold the keys of death
and Hades" (1:17–19). Yet, when in the course of the bewildering sequence of images we hear not only the voice
of the Victor but actually see him, it is almost an anti-

climax. For when the "King of kings and Lord of lords" appears he is "a Lamb with the marks of slaughter upon him" (5:6 passim). The Victor appears as the Victim. The same is true of the church. Now that the decisive victory has been won in heaven, now that there is no more place for the great red dragon in the presence of Christ, the victorious Victim, the dragon is thrown down on the earth. So it was seen by the seer John who described it to us in that most dramatic chapter of the whole Bible, Revelation 12. When the child (that is Jesus) was snatched up to God and his throne, away from the open mouth of the dragon who wanted to devour it, "war broke out in heaven. Michael and his angels waged war upon the dragon. The dragon and his angels fought, but they had not the strength to win, and no foothold was left them in heaven. So the great dragon was thrown down, that serpent of old that led the whole world astray, whose name is Satan, or the Devil—thrown down to the earth, and his angels with him. Then"—so John continues—"I heard a voice in heaven proclaiming aloud: 'This is the hour of victory for our God, the hour of his sovereignty and power, when his Christ comes to his rightful rule! For the accuser of our brothers is overthrown, who day and night accused them before our God. By the sacrifice of the Lamb they have conquered him, and by the testimony which they uttered; for they did not hold their lives too dear to lay them down. Rejoice then, you heavens and you that dwell in them! But woe to you, earth and sea, for the Devil has come down to you in great fury, knowing that his time is short!' " (12:7–12).

This is the situation of the militant church according to John's vision. Christians are attacked from every side. The witnesses of God are defeated and killed (11:7), for the beast who serves the dragon is "allowed to wage war on

God's people and to defeat them" (13:7). While the sons of light of the War Scroll are victorious, the militant church becomes a victim. Indeed, in the book of Revelation the church appears mainly as the company of the martyrs (7:9–17), and the early church was soon going to consider the martyrs as the most genuine soldiers of Christ. Yet their situation is vastly more hopeful than that of the soldiers of the War Scroll, who can only look forward to a victory of wrath. The militant church looks back to the decisive victory at the cross, can therefore endure in the midst of defeat and look forward to the day when Christ will no more be the King incognito but will manifestly make all things new (21:1–5). While the soldiers of the War Scroll seem triumphant victors who at the end are pitifully defeated, Christians are victorious victims. When on their mission of peace everything seems to fail they still keep their serenity and humor. Their task is not to fight the wars of God. Christ and his angels have long ago accomplished this. Their mission is to witness to the victory of Christ who is our peace and to stand fast in all the attacks by powers and principalities. They need not be deadly serious, like the beasts of the Revelation or the soldiers in the Qumrân document. In the midst of distress they are "surprised by joy." The devil knows that his time is short, therefore he fights so furiously. The Christians, however, have received eternal life.

All this may sound far-fetched and meaningless to those who live in an economy of abundance where it is quite respectable to be a Christian. But to the apostles and many Christians since, this vision of world history has imparted meaning without which they could not have fulfilled their mission. The glorious end of Romans, chapter 8, shows this more clearly than any other passage: "If God is on our

side, who is against us? . . . Then what can separate us from
the love of Christ? Can affliction or hardship? Can persecution, hunger, nakedness, peril, or the sword? . . . in spite
of all, overwhelming victory [literally, a "hyper-victory"] is
ours through him who loved us." The success of the soldiers
of the War Scroll proved to be failure, but the failure of the
militant church becomes a hyper-victory.

4. A last significant difference between the Qumrân document and the Bible must be seen. The army of the War
Scroll is under the absolute rule of the priests who remain
behind the front line in order not to get dirty hands. No
one dares proceed before the priests have blown the trumpet
for advance and no one dares throw his spear or shoot his
arrow before the appropriate trumpets are sounded (1QM
viii–ix)! Every move and position is strictly prescribed by
the priests, every detail fixed, including the age of officers,
soldiers and cooks, and not forgetting even the approximate
location of the water closet (1QM vii:7). All this is an adult
male affair, for it is prescribed that "no toddling child or
woman is to enter their camps from the moment they leave
Jerusalem to go to war until they return" (1QM vii:3). On
the whole the fighting of that army seems rather mechanical
and its soldiers are like wheels and cogs in a machine.

The mission of peace on which the militant church is
sent, however, needs mature soldiers who are able to form
their own judgment. They do not live and work according
to a fixed set of principles; rather, in a constant process of
renewal of their ability and criteria of judgment they are
enabled "to discern the will of God, and to know what is
good, acceptable, and perfect" (Rom. 12:2). The militant
church cannot act according to blueprints. It must constantly change its tactics to meet the varying attacks of the

powers and principalities. The mission of peace is full of surprises, an adventure rather than the painstaking carrying out of fixed five-year-plans. In this mission of peace youths and women are not excluded. On the contrary, in the early church, and ever since, the role of Christian women has been of importance. This was so obvious, and in a sense so infuriating, that Libanius, a pagan philosopher, suddenly interrupted his work on a scholarly treatise against the Christian doctrine and exclaimed: "Heavens! What women you Christians have!" He had every reason to speak thus, for in the church's expansion from Jerusalem to the world's capital, Rome, women are foremost in the nucleus of first believers in almost every city. Some of the most moving accounts of the early church's mission describe their steadfast faith and witness. Already by the close of the first century the militant church had infiltrated into Caesar's household, through a woman, of course! Not a few of these Christian women became martyrs, soldiers of Christ who accomplished their mission of peace by giving their lifeblood.[12]

II.

After this comparison between the army of the War Scroll and the militant church we will again draw some conclusions for the ministry of the whole church and its ministers today. All along we have dealt with the apostolicity of the church and the question of apostolic succession, although this was done in terms which do not fit the traditional theological literature on this subject. When we hear the term "apostolic succession" we usually think first of dry volumes in which Catholic and Protestant theologians dispute about how one bishop succeeds another and what this means or does not mean for the authority of the ministers in the church. But we must learn again that apostolic succession has first of all something to do with the continuation of a mission.[13]

The apostles were the pioneers[14] at the front of the militant church, sent on this mission of peace we have come to know in this chapter. Having been eye-witnesses of the victory of Christ, they were personally commissioned by the Lord after his enthronement. "Full authority in heaven and on earth has been committed to me. Go forth therefore and make all nations my disciples" (Matt. 28:18–20). The disciples became ambassadors. In their apostolic witness now contained in the New Testament they have given us the *procès-verbal,* the written evidence, of Christ's victory. To this we can add nothing and from it take nothing away. By giving the authentic witness so that this *procès-verbal* could be written, the apostles had a unique and untransmittable function.

In addition to exercising this unique function the apostles began two missions which had to continue after their death, which are now in process and which will continue until the end of time: (1) the apostolic mission to the world, and (2) the apostolic mission to the church.

1. *The apostolic mission to the world* is fulfilled by the whole church and all its members. By virtue of his baptism each Christian stands in this basic apostolic succession. A recent report of a theological commission on Faith and Order states: "It is the continuity of the redeemed life of the Church in Christ which is the heart of the apostolic succession, or continuity in the apostolically founded Church. Hence through baptism all members partake in the apostolic succession, all share in the one apostolic mission."[15] This mission to the world consists of the following:[16]

(a) The victorious but still hidden heavenly King must be represented in the whole inhabited world, which is still like an occupied country in the power of an already defeated enemy who knows that his time is short. (b) The Lord's victory and his coming triumphal entry must be heralded to all men. (c) Signs of the peace and reconciliation which were wrought by the Victor when at the cross he became the Victim must be erected everywhere. (d) In doing all this the ambassadors have to pay part of the cost of this peace by their suffering.

a) Each layman and lay woman—and the church as a whole—has to *represent* Christ. We are not like cogs in machines set in motion by priests, like the soldiers of the War Scroll. All the baptized have the priestly ministry of representation. The worship of a congregation, a saint's life in the midst of the secular world, a service done in Christ's name: all these are spontaneous representations of Christ no less important than the official representations through the words and acts of especially ordained ministers in the fulfilment of their office. In order to be a representative we must on the one hand remain in intimate communion with him who sent us. Just as the first Christians, we too must meet "constantly to hear the apostles teach, and to share the common life, to break bread and to pray" (Acts 2:42). On the other hand, we must go wherever our Lord sends us and be present where he wants us to be, and that is in the world, with its power politics. There the battles of faith have to be fought so that the idols of the twentieth century will be smashed and man be freed to live a truly human life. It is not those Christians who spend most of their spare time in church buildings and church organizations who are therefore "key laymen," but those men and women who seek enough spiritual food and exercise in the camps

of the militant church that they can truly represent Christ
at the place where they live and work, that they can be
present with Christ at their particular position at the front.

b) The apostolic mission is no silent representation. The
victory has to be *heralded*. This is not the task of a few pro-
fessionals. Every Christian receives the sword which the
Spirit gives, namely the words that come from God (Eph.
6:17). The sword of God's word need not always be used
to preach sermons. It is far more effective when Christians
spontaneously "gossip the gospel" to their neighbors and
colleagues. It is amazing how much one can say if one does
not preach from without or from above, but from within,
as one who is fully present in a given group.[17] Summing up
the studies on the missionary outreach of the early church,
T. W. Manson wrote:

> The Christianity that conquered the Roman Empire was
> not an affair of brilliant preachers addressing packed con-
> gregations. We have, so far as I know, nothing much in the
> way of brilliant preachers in the first three hundred years
> of the Church's life. There were one or two brilliant contro-
> versialists, but I suspect that they made more enemies than
> friends; and the greatest of them all, Origen, was probably
> over the heads of most people most of the time. The great
> preachers came after Constantine the Great; and before that
> Christianity had already done its work and made its way
> right through the Empire from end to end. When we try to
> picture how it was done we seem to see domestic servants
> teaching Christ in and through their domestic service,
> workers doing it through their work, small shopkeepers
> through their trade, and so on, rather than eloquent prop-
> agandists swaying mass meetings of interested inquirers.[18]

c) The heralding is intimately linked with the third
element of the apostolic mission, the *erection of signs of
peace*. When God speaks, it happens; when he acts, he explains. The Old Testament word used in this connection is

dabar, which means both the word and the event. So it must be also with God's people. Whoever speaks about peace and quarrels with his brothers and neighbors is not trustworthy. Whoever preaches love and does not see and respond to the needs of the world in which he lives is a hypocrite. Our apostolic ministry of representation and of heralding must be accompanied by such deeds, acts and realities as illustrate our message of peace and give our words authority in the ears of the hearers. When speaking about these signs of peace we tend to think first of spectacular Christian social action programs, mission hospitals, rural reconstruction, etc. These can indeed be important signs, but there are others which may be less spectacular but more effective. "The lives of Christians will have to be the parables of the Kingdom for the twentieth century."[19] Something must therefore be done about the latent schizophrenia of the church, the split life where on Sunday morning we confess Christ and on Monday adore Mammon, where in baptism we accept the risk of failure and in daily work make success our God, where in Holy Communion we come to the very heart of peace, while in international, racial and social relationships we continue cold war. This schizophrenia cannot, of course, be healed by moralistic sermons from the pulpit. The priestly people of the militant church are not allowed to remain behind the battle-line in order not to soil their hands, as was the case with the priests in the army of the War Scroll. To represent Christ one must be present in the midst of the hard struggles of this world, and Christians will therefore always get dirty hands and will constantly have to live in compromise. But what do we do with our dirty hands? Our tendency is to cover them with the gloves of religiosity. The sign of peace, however, is to confess our sin, to accept God's forgiveness for our neighbors and ourselves, to fight all cheap and irresponsible compromises and to work in each situation for the costly responsible compromise. Another mighty sign of peace is the unity of the church—not just the unity in doctrine, in the celebration of sacraments and in ecclesiastical structures, but above all the unity of Christians in the social structures of their daily life and work. The struggle for this unity at the frontier is commissioned to all laymen by virtue of the basic apostolic succession into which they have been ordained at their baptism.

d) The comparison between the militant church and the army of the War Scroll has clearly shown that the mission of peace through the representation of the King incognito in the world, through the heralding of his victory and the erection of signs of his peace, involves *suffering*. The whole fourth chapter will be devoted to this subject.

2. What must still be seen, however, is the place of especially ordained ministers of the church in the succession of this apostolic mission. The apostles were sent on a mission to the whole world. By virtue of the basic apostolic succession the whole church with all its members continues this mission through its worship and its apostolic life. Yet, the apostles were also entrusted with a mission to the church.[20] This *apostolic mission to the church* is continued throughout the centuries by the life and work of ordained ministers who by virtue of their ordination stand in a special apostolic succession. From a time very early in church history the continuity of this apostolic mission to the church was by many related to episcopal ordination. Such an ordered succession of ordination throughout the centuries is certainly a valuable sign for the continuance of the special apostolic succession, but it does not guarantee this continuance. More important is the actual fulfilment of the apos-

tolic mission to the church. It includes at least the following
three functions: (*a*) the function of pioneering in and for
the church, (*b*) the function of strengthening the church
in its life and mission and (*c*) the function of uniting the
church for its task in the world.

a) Like the apostles the apostolic ministers are called to
be *pioneers*. In Western Christendom and in its predomi-
nant conceptions about what ministers are and do, probably
too one-sided an emphasis has been laid on the pastoral and
leadership functions at the expense of the distinctive functions exercised by the pioneers and missionaries of the
church. Like the apostle Paul many ministers must today
cross frontiers and go as ambassadors of Christ into new
areas and eras. This pioneer function of apostolic ministers
does not release all other members of the apostolic church
from being pioneering witnesses wherever they go. In fact
many churches in Asia and Africa began to grow not as the
result of organized missionary work but due to the spontaneous witness of Western and indigenous laymen who
happened to come to these areas because of their secular
work.[21] Nevertheless, from a time very early in church history, some members of the apostolic church were especially
set apart for such a pioneer ministry. It was a wrong development when in the missionary movement of the last centuries the total mission seemed to be conceived almost
exclusively in terms of the service of such specially designated pioneer ministers and in terms of their missionary
activities and institutions. Yet the modern vogue of writing
off all such missionaries and to speak only of the spontaneous
witness of the laity is also one-sided. Often the example set
by pioneer missionaries has led to a missionary awakening
of a total church (a modern instance is the deep impact of
the short-lived pioneer work of the worker priests on the

French Roman Catholic church). Apostolic ministers have to pioneer so that the whole apostolic church may fulfil its pioneer task.

b) As soon as the apostolic presence of pioneer ministers results in the enlistment of new troops of the militant church in a given new area or time, the pioneer ministers receive the additional task of *strengthening* the nascent church. As Peter and Paul were appointed "to lend strength" to the church (Luke 22:32; Acts 18:32), so all ministers are called to do the same. This work of strengthening includes, first of all, continuous intercession for the church. "Continually I make mention of you in my prayers," wrote Paul to the Christians in Rome; and in Colossians 1:28–29 he added in a compact way what else belongs to that strengthening mission: "He it is whom we proclaim. We admonish everyone without distinction, we instruct everyone in all the ways of wisdom, so as to present each one of you as a mature member of Christ's body. To this end I am toiling strenuously with all the energy and power of Christ at work in me." One could write an excellent pastoral theology simply by explaining this passage word by word. We should add that certainly also the administration of the sacraments belongs to this strengthening function of apostolic ministers, although in the New Testament it is never explicitly said that only ordained ministers should administer sacraments. Again, the strengthening function of apostolic ministers does not release other members of the apostolic church from fulfilling their own ministry of intercession, teaching and mutual pastoral care. On the contrary, the apostolic ministers are given as the pastors for a pastoral church, as teachers for a teaching church, as preachers for a witnessing church.

c) Finally, the apostolic ministers are, like the apostles and the whole apostolic church, entrusted with *the concern for unity*. They have to continue the process of fitting one stone to the other in the building process of the church which began with Peter (Matt. 16:18) and to which Paul devoted his whole life. To build with "living stones" which tend to roll away is no easy task. This may be a reason why so many ministers today escape to far easier building programs with dead bricks and mortar. Yet such is not their primary calling. Like Paul they have to devote all their strength to build up the church, uniting it for its apostolic life in the world.

When ministers serve the church in this pioneering, strengthening and uniting way, the whole church will be fit to fulfil its apostolic mission of peace. Without the continuation of this mission of peace the specific apostolic succession is nothing. Yet without the strenuous toiling of apostolic ministers in their mission to the church the basic apostolic succession of the whole church withers away.

One thing becomes clear at the end of this chapter: it is totally wrong when ministers ask lay people, "Won't you help the church?" This betrays an introverted view. The church is then conceived mainly as consisting of church activities, buildings and all that busy ministers plan. And the ministers look then rather like the priests in the army of the War Scroll. The apostolic perspective becomes right only when laymen begin to ask their ministers, "Won't you help us, the church, so that we may become fit for our mission of peace?"

3

EQUIPPED FOR GRACIOUS
SERVICE

As one might expect, the soldiers of the Roman legions were not always content with their pay. This was a dangerous discontentment, because since about the time of the Emperor Augustus Roman politics were more and more influenced by the Roman army. Augustus himself acknowledged this fact when he began the impressive account of his deeds, now known as his testament, with the words: "At the age of nineteen I mobilized an army of my own free will and by my own means. With this army I gave back freedom to the state which had been oppressed by the tyranny of a party." The rulers of Rome had to satisfy the insatiable demand of the Roman plebes for bread and circuses, and even the mighty Augustus was compelled to buy popularity in this way. "Three times in my own name and five times in the name of my sons and grandsons I organized fights of gladiators. Around ten thousand men fought in these combats." "In the thirteenth year of my consulate [2 B.C.] I instituted for the first time the festival of Mars which was thereafter organized by the consuls. Twenty-six times I ordered that in my own name and the name of my sons and grandsons hunts of African animals be organized in the circus, the forum and the amphitheatres, in which about thirty-five hundred wild animals were used." This is only a short quotation out of a long list in Augustus's

testament.[1] We see that the grandiose theater of the later
persecutions and sufferings of Christians, which will be the
subject of the next chapter, was already waiting. What in-
terests us now in these lists of Augustus's liberalities is the
fact that not only the Roman plebes are mentioned as the
recipients, but also the army. The greater the influence of
the army, the more it had to be pacified by such free gifts,
by a *donativum* or—to use the Greek term—a *charisma*.
Sulla, the dictator, and the consul Pompey had already begun
to distribute gold among the legionaries in the early part
of the first century B.C. Augustus, who died in the year A.D.
14, initiated the custom of granting such free gifts to the
army over and above their regular pay not only at victory
celebrations but also on the occasion of joyous events in his
family. Later every emperor was expected to distribute such
free gifts when he came to the throne and each year on his
birthday. These were moments of rejoicing in the Roman
army, for the gifts became larger and larger. In the third
century of our era the gold coins distributed had reached
the size of a small plate.[2]

The militant church too knows such days of rejoicing
when it receives free gifts or *charismata*. At the celebration
of baptism new members receive the state of grace. At the
feast of the Lord's Supper their state of grace is renewed
and strengthened. But more than that, the militant church
lives continuously in this joy because there is a constant
flow of *charismata* from God to his church. Paul said this
once in a very forceful way in the same chapter in which
he spoke about baptism and about the fact that each baptized Christian has to put himself totally at the disposal of
God, letting his body not become a weapon for sin but a
weapon for doing right. "For"—so Paul ended this argument
—"sin pays a wage, and the wage is death, but God gives

freely, and his gift is eternal life, in union with Christ Jesus our Lord" (Rom. 6:23). Paul used here the technical terms for military pay and that free gift to the army about which I have just spoken. Sin promises and actually pays an *opsonion*,[3] pay which should suffice for the livelihood of its soldiers; but this wage is death. Sin is a liar; it promises life and gives death. Just as each wage is paid not once only but repeatedly, so also is that of sin. As soldiers of sin we live, even now, constantly in the atmosphere of death. Yet this is what we deserve, what is lawfully paid to us. As the militant church, however, we live not by merit, but by grace. At baptism we have been transplanted from the area of merit with its stench of make-believe and corruption into the domain of grace with its foretaste of real life, the life eternal in communion with Christ.

I.

It was Paul who introduced the term *charisma* into the Christian vocabulary.[4] In the following we shall (1) make a quick survey of the occurrences and the meaning of this term in the New Testament epistles; (2) see how this charismatic equipment marks the life and ministry of the church; and (3) examine the spiritual armor as described in Ephesians 6:10–18.

1. Most famous are the lists of gifts of grace contained in the letters to the Christians in Rome and Corinth,[5] where the *charismata* mean specific things, in part quite unspectacular and down-to-earth gifts such as those of administration, teaching, leadership, of wise speech and sound knowledge, but also quite unexpected gifts which take the church by surprise such as those of miraculous powers, proph-

ecy and of ecstatic utterances, more commonly known as the
gift of speaking in tongues. Besides these special *charismata*
Paul used the same term also for designating all that God
did for us in the great history of salvation (Rom. 5:15f.;
11:29) or in our personal life, such as the gift of the un-
married or married state (I Cor. 7:7). Paul even used the
word of God's coming to his rescue in a dangerous situation
(II Cor. 1:8—11). Later, in the time of the pastoral letters, the
charismata were also linked with the special ordination of
ministers of the church (I Tim. 4:14; II Tim. 1:6).

It is good to distinguish these different understandings
of the term, but one must not separate them, for all have
the same root, namely, God's free grace. There are in fact
far more charismatic manifestations in the life of the church
and its members than are actually designated by the technical term in the New Testament. Therefore instead of setting
up artificial lists and classifications of *charismata* it is better
to sharpen our eyes for what distinguishes the charismatic
from the non-charismatic or—to say the same thing in other
biblical terms—to distinguish the Holy Spirit from the rebellious powers and principalities. Only through this discernment of the spirits, which itself is a *charisma* (I Cor.
12:10), can we be and remain the militant church. For only
then do we know whether we are God's soldiers who join
in his mission of peace or deserters who immediately also
become *theomachoi*, "people who are at war with God"
(Acts 5:39), because there is no neutrality in this spiritual
struggle. One lives either by merit or by grace. To those
who, like the Christians in Galatia, find after all that grace
is not sufficient and seek additional security in merit under
the law, Paul writes severely: "When you seek to be justified
by way of law, your relation with Christ is completely

severed: you have fallen out of the domain of God's grace"
(Gal. 5:4).

What then are the criteria for judging whether we live
by grace or not? How can the *charismata* be discerned? One
clue for answering this question can be found at the beginning of the famous twelfth chapter of I Corinthians. There
Paul used three terms in a complementary, almost inter-
changeable way, namely the terms (*a*) *charisma* which means
a gift originating in God's free grace, (*b*) *pneumatika,* which
are the gifts of the Holy Spirit which manifest themselves
in *energemata,* i.e., in the energy and operation of the Spirit,
(*c*) *diakonia* which means humble service according to the
pattern laid down by Christ. Wherever this origination in
God's grace, this manifestation of the energy of the Spirit
and this Christlike service are present, there is *charisma.*
Paul suggests thus a dynamic conception of *charisma* which
is far better adapted for discerning the right equipment of
a fighting army than the static and legalistic concepts which
many later theologians have elaborated. A so-called natural
endowment can then become a *charisma* if this endowment
is understood and used according to the three criteria mentioned earlier. Or a so-called supra-natural gift may well
have been given as a *charisma,* but when accepted with
pride, manipulated for egoistic purposes and used for domi-
neering over others, it loses its character as a *charisma.*

2. Only those gifts, abilities and events belong to the
right equipment of the militant church which are (*a*) received as coming from God's grace, (*b*) administered as
energy of the Holy Spirit and (*c*) directed towards Christlike service. Under those three aspects we will now see how
this equipment of grace marks the church.

a) No Christian merits or owns this equipment of grace. It is given to him and received by him as a trust, whose steward he becomes. While from God's side these gifts of grace are irrevocable, their stewards may never neglect them but must constantly seek them and stir them into flames.[6] The *charismata* come to us, become manifest through us and change our very being, but we never become their owners. They are not at our disposal according to our own will and for our own purpose. Nobody really likes this. It is too adventurous. We would like to have stable, secure items on which we can definitely count. We like to possess things, even such things as salvation and faith. Once in East Berlin I met a group of Christians who told me about their evangelistic house visitations to convinced and well-trained atheists. First, they went there full of vigor, being certain of their own faith and possession of truth. But in their conversations with the atheists they lost one argument after the other and their witness made no impact at all. This went so far that they themselves began to doubt the very existence of God. All their arguments and certainties had been knocked out of their hands. Yet, compelled by God, they continued to visit the homes of the atheists. They came now with empty hands, with a mixture of doubts and belief. Then things began to happen. Atheists recognized that these Christians did not come to sell an ideology but that they were sent by someone who apparently could use even failures. Today there are house-churches in several of the homes of these former atheists. Christians are not fit to be sent on God's mission as long as they live by the merit of their own certainties. As long as we believe in our own belief, our own denomination, our own ready-made answers and remedies, we cannot be soldiers of the militant church. For if we go on a mission with hands full of certainties to distribute to poor pre- or post-Christian pagans, we may well serve, but in a paternalistic way, not graciously as our Lord did, and ultimately we will then serve our own self-gratification.

b) The equipment is a spiritual one: that means it is a manifestation of the power of the Holy Spirit. Already the Christians in Corinth, and since then whole churches, misunderstood this manifestation of the Spirit. They tended to equate *charismata* with extraordinary enthusiasm and ecstasy. There are indeed such *charismata,* especially among first generation Christians and among revival movements.[7] However, neither the abundance nor the lack of enthusiastic and ecstatic manifestations is a true measure for the charismatic state of the church. Where there is charismatic enthusiasm such as faith healing, prophecy and speaking in tongues one may rejoice in it. Yet one must carefully examine whether this enthusiasm is not a manifestation of godless powers and principalities,[8] and one must seek also such often far more important yet less spectacular *charismata* as wisdom and discernment. Where there is little or no charismatic enthusiasm one may seek it, but then not despise such down-to-earth gifts as administration and leadership. A lack of charismatic enthusiasm often leads to spiritual dullness, church bureaucracy and fear of risks. Abundance of charismatic enthusiasm, however, engenders often sectarianism and spiritual authoritarianism.[9] The measure with which all manifestations of the Spirit will have to be checked is that indicated by Paul to the Corinthians: "No one can say 'Jesus is Lord!' except under the influence of the Holy Spirit" (I Cor. 12:3). He referred of course not just to a thoughtless babbling of this formula but to a real confession which marks our whole way of life. All our spiritual heritage, our spiritual achievements and our whole

spirituality will therefore constantly have to be submitted to
the following question: Does this manifestation of the
Spirit lead to self-aggrandizement or to the confession of
Christ as Lord, and this in such a way that those who confess Christ follow him in taking on the form of a servant?

c) Gifts which originate in God's grace and whose nature
manifests the power of the Holy Spirit have therefore all
one and the same purpose: *diakonia*. They mold us into
the form of the Servant. One cannot store *charismata* for
possible later use. They are given to be spent. It is note-
worthy that all major *charismata* lists in the New Testament
occur in connection with texts about the church as the body
of Christ and lead up to a call for true Christian love. No
charisma is thus given just for one individual only, for his
self-edification. All are given for the building up of the
total body (I Cor. 12:7; 14:3–5) in love and service to our
brothers and neighbors (Rom. 12:9–13:10). The *charismata*
are therefore intimately inter-related like the members of
an orchestra. Some may have quite unique instruments,
others may play together in a group of the same or similar
instruments, but all are dependent on one another. Each
must await his right time[10] for playing and all must be
sensitive to one another, otherwise the result will be a
cacophony instead of a symphony. Such a disorder apparently reigned among the Christians in Corinth. Not only
did they overestimate charismatic enthusiasm but their
charismata had somehow run wild, a thing which appeared
of course especially in their worship gatherings. We are
those who profit from their chaos, for because of it Paul
wrote those marvellous three chapters about the *charismata*
in I Corinthians which contain not only the pearl of the
hymn of love in chapter 13 but also this glimpse of early
Christian worship which shows better than any theological

treatise how the charismatic equipment marks the militant church. "When you meet for worship, each of you contributes a hymn, some instruction, a revelation, an ecstatic utterance, or the interpretation of such an utterance. All of these must aim at one thing: to build up the church" (14:26).

3. All this sounds a little too harmless if one forgets that this charismatic equipment is given for combat. Those Christians who after the military oath of their baptism have gone on permanent leave, coming back only for an occasional show of the *militia Christi,* and those who unconsciously have become deserters, need no such charismatic equipment. They can happily live on with the merit of their religiosity and their so-called Christian principles. But Timothy, for instance, was fighting and therefore he was told: "Take strength from the grace of God which is ours in Christ Jesus;" then you can "take your share of hardship, like a good soldier of Christ Jesus" (II Tim. 2:1, 3). Similarly, all Christians need to put on the spiritual armor of God, "for our fight is not against human foes, but against cosmic powers, against the authorities and potentates of this dark world, against the superhuman forces of evil in the heavens" (Eph. 6:12). When discussing what baptism means and on what kind of a mission we are sent, we came to know these powers and principalities. Let us now have a more careful look at the spiritual armor given for the combat with them.[11]

Whoever wrote the famous passage in Ephesians 6:10–18, with its most complete description of the armor of God, must have been well acquainted with the Roman army, for he used the technical military terms in an accurate way. What astonishes one, however, is the omission of offensive weapons. The Christian needs no lance or spear, no bow and arrows, which were an integral part of the Roman armor. He needs not even the long battle sword. The sword mentioned in Ephesians 6:17 is actually only a dagger.[12] The defensive parts of the full military armor suffice because the decisive advance into the territory of the enemy and the decisive combat have already been won by Christ. The task of the militant church is now to stand firm as God's colony in the world and from the base of this colony to go on that apostolic mission of peace described in the last chapter. The mere presence of the church in the world is a strong attack on the still remaining power and authority of devilish forces. No wonder, therefore, that the church comes immediately under attack. Several times texts from the Old Testament are hinted at in Ephesians 6 which describe how God puts on his full armor in order to fight for his people and to lend them the cover of his shield.[13]

This cover is more than necessary, because the attacks of what Paul called the powers and principalities are very subtle. It belongs to their very essence that they remain invisible, that they manifest themselves only in disguise, for instance through existing political and social structures, through sex or religion—all things which were created by God for a good purpose. Their main weapon is the lie. They have a subtle way of falsifying reality, of giving everything the appearance of temptation and then the smell of corruption. Things which do not matter are blown up to an almost grotesque importance while those things which really matter are minimized and hidden. Like the Roman soldier who in arming himself first buckled on an apron for his loins, the soldier of Christ must first of all buckle on the apron of truth. In the context of the whole passage of Ephesians 6, "truth" means not subjective truthfulness but the objective truth of reality. In the struggle of the Christian

life the first task is to perceive what really matters, to come
to know the true reality of a given person, thing or situation,
and to free oneself from the corrupted images which hidden
persuaders constantly impute to us. Neither shallow pessi-
mism nor optimism is our calling, but a deep respect for
the realities of life. Christian spirituality is far more a
spirituality of true objectivity (*Sachlichkeit*) than of ideal-
ism. To see and deal with things, persons and situations in
their true reality, namely that which comes from God and
for which God has destined them, is our task. This means
that a Christian constantly demythologizes himself and the
world around him. A cartoonist should sometime draw the
Christian as a person with a small pin in his hand going
through the world of blown-up phantom reality fabricated
by hidden persuaders and sticking his pin in all the balloons
of personal, national and racial pride, of lies, myths and
propaganda. Then the balloons would disappear, shrieking
with great noise, and one would see the truth of the matter.

Another of the tactics of the hidden persuaders is their
subtle insistence that man needs more than grace. He must
live by merit, the merit of his good works, of his status, his
religiosity or whatever else the persuaders choose to misuse
for their purpose. Therefore, each soldier of Christ has to
put on righteousness as a breastplate. This is, of course, not
that abominable self-righteousness of Christians and so-
called "Christian nations" which look down from their tower
of pride on people of other faiths or no faith. It is the righteousness in the eyes of God which Christ gained for us when
he became the victorious victim at the cross, the same righteousness which made history when Martin Luther redis-
covered it in his struggle for the right understanding of
Paul's letters to the Romans and Galatians.

Being so armed against the insidious atmosphere of lies

and pride the militant church attacks—with peace. In the last chapter we already saw the paradox of an army fighting with the gospel of peace, of a peace which is not the "take-it-easy" peace, but the sign for going on a mission. This gospel of peace is first of all addressed to men, while according to some texts the destiny of the rebellious powers and principalities seems ultimately to be destruction (I Cor. 15:24–28). Yet there are other texts, especially in the letters to the Ephesians and Colossians, which speak about a cosmic peace, a total reconciliation, where not only individuals, but whole social structures, in fact all powers and principalities are brought under Christ's domination. "Through him God chose to reconcile the whole universe to himself, making peace through the shedding of his blood upon the cross— to reconcile all things, whether on earth or in heaven, through him alone" (Col. 1:20). Here "the things in heaven," which is a way of speaking about the powers and principalities, are not destroyed[14] but dethroned and disarmed. Later in the same letter to the Colossians the cosmic powers and principalities appear as captives in the triumphal procession of Christ (2:15), just as defeated kings were made showpieces when during their triumphal entry the victorious Roman generals and emperors led them into Rome. Powers and principalities are in themselves not demonic. They were created by God in whose creation they fulfil important functions. They have been corrupted—like man. But now the gospel of peace is also addressed to them. The mission of peace and therefore the ministry of all baptized has not only personal and international, but also cosmic scope.

Through the offensive by means of the gospel of peace the combat reaches its height. In the armor of the Christian again two purely defensive weapons are therefore mentioned: the great shield of faith and the helmet of salvation.

During their marches the Roman soldiers carried their helmets hung on a string. As soon as the order came to put on the helmets they knew that combat was about to begin. For Christians the combat has indeed begun. A shrewd device of powers and principalities is to alienate man and his daily life from God. The hidden persuaders separate God's love from God's justice, so that they can accuse us and give us a constantly bad conscience. Or they try to replace the reality of God who is the Lord of world history with the emasculated image of a god who would be interested only in religion and who would spend most of his time in church activities. Or they try to convince us that there is no God. Therefore the shield of faith is needed, not just the subjective virtue of faithfulness or the external acceptance of a creed but that mighty faith which, against all deceitful external evidence, holds fast to the sure love of God for us and for the whole universe. However contrary or weak the external evidence of salvation may be, the salvation of the world and of myself has been wrought by Christ. In the parallel text in I Thessalonians 5:8 Paul spoke about the helmet of the hope of salvation. This hopeful looking forward to the visible manifestation of the salvation of the world is meant also in Ephesians 6.

Finally again two more active things are mentioned: the dagger of the Spirit which is the word of God, and that other most important weapon of every Christian, prayer. For a modern man living in our day of inflated words these two sound rather like an anticlimax. Yet the reference here is not to our words about God. Most parts of most of our sermons, our theological books (alas, also this book!) and our witness to non-Christians are nothing more than such pale and indeed helpless words about God. We deceive ourselves if we believe that much is done by them. It may

actually be a device of the deceiving powers to let laymen
and ministers have the illusion that a word spoken in the
pulpit or during an evangelism campaign should have an
almost magic effect. It simply has not. What completes the
spiritual armor is not such words *about* God. It is, first of
all, the words *of* God, the *dabar,* which are, at the same time,
word and event and which happen to us and all men, and
sometimes through us, in the most unlikely situations. On
the other hand, they are the words *to* God which we address
to him in prayers, supplications and intercessions.

II.

All through this biblical exposition of the charismatic
equipment of the militant church and of its spiritual armor
there were points where one would have liked to stop, to
give illustrations and to show implications for today. Let
us now see at least a few of these conclusions. They concern
(1) the charismatic way of life and ministry of the militant
church. In this context (2) some more things will also have
to be said about the ministers of the charismatic church.

1. The spiritual equipment gives the militant church its
particular *charismatic way of life* or spirituality. The church
is a continuous Pentecost, a body of people who each day
receive anew the new life in Christ through the Spirit. Those
who have merited death receive eternal life, those who have
earned the wages of sin receive a continuous flow of free
gifts of grace. Moreover, they receive these gifts in a most
gracious way. God does not give as we usually give, namely
with words such as: "Really you did not deserve this, but
I am giving it to you all the same." God does not give in
this humiliating way, with strings and stings attached. When

at the last judgment Christ gives the beloved of his Father the greatest gift, the entry into God's kingdom, he actually thanks them. He accepts whatever they have done to the least of mankind as a service rendered to him (Matt. 25: 34–36). He thanks when he gives. This is the pattern of gracious service. The dominant note in true Christian spirituality is therefore neither pride in being a Christian nor the crusader's spirit which always wants to do something for God, but wonder and joy (Matt. 25:37–39). Worship is its first expression, worship not just as a duty or as a preparation for the subsequent mission, but worship for God's sake, worship in which we sing, praise and pray as God's children.

The *charismata* free us from the curse of a life by our own merit and self-justification, be it as lonely individuals who pathetically create their own world or as members in a crowd who apathetically conform to set patterns. Both in that lonely individual and this member of a crowd true man is lost. The *charismata,* however, give us back our true self. They recover personality and community at the same time: grace is never given in general, but always to me or to you as a special *charisma* (Rom. 12:3, 6). Everyone who was incorporated and ordained through baptism in the militant church is therefore irreplaceable and indispensable. This frees us from having constantly to compare ourselves with others. There is no more place for superiority complexes, but neither for inferiority complexes. These complexes, especially the "Christian" ones, are nothing else than a subtle form of immaturity and unbelief. The *charismata* give us worth as a person, yet at the same time they insert us in a community. The same grace which gives personality incorporates. This frees us from the curse of having to do everything, and to accomplish it alone. Grace assigns to me and to you our God-given place and limits. There is a great blessing in this being able finally to accept our limits in a given time and place and for a given task, instead of being constantly chased by ambition to the ultimately sterile rush of doing and wanting too much too quickly.

Yet while grace grants us the serenity which comes from accepting our God-given place and limits, at the same time it gives us power to grow far beyond our natural limitations. We need no longer live as immature slaves under the rigid tutorship of the law, be it a religious law or the law of conformity. We are freed from the tyranny of the "musts" or "must nots" and can grow into that glorious freedom of God's sons who are enabled to judge for themselves and who in each new situation discern what is the will of God. We are now *theodidaktoi,* i.e., people who are taught by God himself in the wisdom of love (I Thess. 4:9). The Christian community on all its levels, from the house-church to the world-wide Christian fellowship, is the place of this growth into maturity. Our brothers and sisters in Christ, who are often quite tiresome people, are given to us.[15] We cannot choose them according to our own liking. This sometimes rather queer colony of God becomes thus the training ground for the militant church; here its soldiers learn patience, mutual submission, forgiveness and love. There they are trained to accept God-given limits, to wait for the God-given right time and to use their gifts of grace for the common good.

The result of all this is what Dietrich von Oppen has called *Frömmigkeit als Sachlichkeit,* spirituality as true objectivity.[16] Objectivity must here of course not be taken as a cold and impersonal attitude, but as a deep respect for the truth of reality. This kind of objectivity helps and heals situations and relationships. Facts are then no longer either adored or ignored. Man, human society and the processes and products of both nature and technology are then seen as parts of God's creation, marked by corruption but also by the impact of God's grace. Gracious service means then to help this creation to achieve its true purpose.

One could sum this up spiritually also with the New Testament conception of mature manhood. While the powers and principalities want to make us things, or beasts, or gods, the spiritual equipment gives us power to grow into mature manhood, to become true human beings within a truly human society. The militant church is thus called to be human, contagiously human.

When considering the ministry of the church one usually thinks about what the church and its members should do or say, what service campaigns and evangelistic crusades should be organized and what should be planned and budgeted for years ahead. Yet the greatest ministry is performed if individual Christians and church communities just live in the charismatic way of life in the world we have been describing, if they worship in wonder and serve with grace. The charismatic equipment gives back to the church what it is always in danger of losing and yet needs so sorely for its combat for peace, namely spontaneity. Ministry is in the first place not all that we organize as Christian service and witness. Such organized church activities can be a good training. They are also an important supplement to the spontaneous ministry if they do not impose themselves in such a way that they suffocate the free manifestations of the Spirit,[17] the manifold spontaneous services rendered within the Christian community (Rom. 12:6–8) and the charismatic flavor with which ordinary work is done (Rom. 12:9—13:10). For, indeed, Christian work is mostly not something special done in addition to our ordinary work, but it is ordinary

work done with grace. This is no call for abolishing all
organized church activities. A certain amount of planning,
organization and institution is quite essential. Without institutional elements the church would soon be a ghost. Far
from being the opposite of the institutional element, the
charismata actually create, give life to and renew institutions.
The question thus is not whether or not the church should
have organized activities and institutions, but how many or
how few and what kind of such activities and institutions a
militant church must have. What activities, budget items
and institutions hinder rather than foster the spontaneous
life and ministry of the church—and must therefore be
buried? What helps or hinders the militant church to go on
its mission of peace, worshiping with wonder and serving
with grace?

2. In the context of this charismatic life and ministry of
the church a new light is also shed on *the ministers of the
charismatic church*. There is an old theological debate about
the relationship between the *charismata* and the offices entrusted to especially ordained ministers. Some define the
authority and function of ordained ministers almost exclusively on the basis of the *charismata,* while others make
a clear-cut distinction between *charismata* and offices of the
church. Both are probably wrong.

In this connection Ephesians 4:7–12 is often mentioned.
This passage begins with the statement that "each of us has
been given his gift, his due portion of Christ's bounty."
This is followed by difficult verses about Christ descending
from heaven to earth and ascending "with captives in his
train," which most probably is a reference to Christ's victory over the cosmic powers. Because Christ has now full
authority, he can distribute gifts. "These were his gifts:

some to be apostles, some prophets, some evangelists, some
pastors and teachers, to equip God's people for work in his
service, to the building up of the body of Christ" (4:11–12).
It is not said here that certain of those baptized have received those *charismata* necessary to be apostles, prophets,
pastors, etc., and that therefore they have been entrusted
with such offices in the church. The people given for fulfilling these functions are themselves the gifts of Christ. Not to
accept them and thus to become anti-clerical would mean
to despise the gifts of Christ. The *charismata* whose stewards
these given men or women happen to be are certainly important. But these *charismata* do not in themselves authorize
their stewards to fulfil an office in the church. Somebody
may indeed have received the most needed *charismata* for
teaching, pastoral care or leadership, but this is not sufficient
reason for him to assert himself as a teacher, pastor or leader
in the church. He may very well be called to teach technology, to become a shop steward or personnel manager in
industry or to be a political leader. Discernment and prophecy are certainly most needed *charismata* for preaching, but
somebody who has been endowed with these may well be
called to become a columnist for international affairs in a
newspaper. The question whether I should serve God and
his creation as God's man in and for the church or as God's
man in and through a secular job is a matter of special
calling rather than of *charismata*. The basic calling to be
God's man or woman and to serve God full time is addressed
to *all* who have been baptized. All have also received varied
charismata. The bad habit of restricting such words as "calling," "God's man," or "full-time Christian service" just to
those who happen to be ministers of the church or on the
payroll of the church is a dangerous way of clericalizing
God, his action and his church. Yet, for the inward and

outward growth of the church, and in view of its mission
of peace, certain things must be done continuously, such as
the pioneer work in areas where there is as yet no church,
the teaching of the gospel, the administration of the sacraments, pastoral oversight, etc. Some church member may
be equipped with the most needed *charismata* for fulfilling
one or several of these necessary functions. The best thing
is then to discern these "given men or women" and to call
them, so that through a special ordination they are set
apart within and for the church to fulfil these functions
with the authority which the special apostolic succession
confers. Both those who call and the one who accepts the
call will then have to be on their guard so that the given
charismata are not neglected. In other cases, however, men
or women must be called and ordained who at the moment
are not equipped with the *charismata* most needed for the
work to be done. In this case the new ministers and the
church which called them will have earnestly to seek the
needed *charismata*. The *charismata* may then follow the
special call instead of preceding it. *Charismata* and offices
in the church can thus neither be wholly identified nor
wholly separated.

More important than this question about *how* the ministers of the church are given is the question *for what* they are
given. Ephesians 4:12 answers: "to equip God's people for
work in his service." Translated in the terms of this chapter
this means that the ministers are given in order that the
militant church may really receive and accept its charismatic
equipment and put on the armor of God, to see that it does
not "fall out of the domain of grace," but grow in grace,
show forth its particular way of life and fulfil its ministry
of gracious service. We see Paul fulfilling exactly this kind
of function in his dealing with the difficult and quarrelsome

church in Corinth. Despite all the trouble and sorrow this particular church had given him, Paul began his first letter to the Corinthians with a prayer of thanksgiving: "I am always thanking God for you. I thank him for his grace given to you in Christ Jesus. I thank him for all the enrichment that has come to you in Christ. . . . There is indeed no single gift [*charisma*] you lack" (1:4–7). Only in this spirit of continuous thanksgiving can ministers really believe that each one baptized has indeed received *charismata*. "Everyone has the gift God has granted him, one this gift and another that" (I Cor. 7:7). It is perhaps the most daring adventure of faith to believe this promise, because the *charismata* given to each one baptized are never obvious. They can be discerned only by eyes opened in continuous thanksgiving. Yet without this belief everything goes wrong. Ministers begin to consider themselves as the only charismatics. They begin to set all the patterns in the church. Then they mobilize the laity for their own plans, teach them their own clericalized image of God, his church and his creation. When suddenly new *charismata* manifest themselves among church members, these ministers get frightened, squeeze the charismatics into the traditional set pattern of church life or force them to emigrate into sects. Paul acted differently. He thanked God for the *charismata,* helped the Corinthians to discern, develop and discipline them, so that indeed this church in Corinth was equipped for gracious service.

4

AN ARMY OF VICTORIOUS
VICTIMS

All those who visit ancient Rome must see the church of
St. Clement, especially what has been discovered beneath it.
This place is in fact an architectural summary of the first
centuries of church history. Beneath St. Clement's the ruins
of a Roman house have been found in which one big room
was apparently used as the meeting place of one of the
several house-churches in Rome.[1] Here a Christian teacher
like Justin Martyr must have taught converts, telling them
about Christ's victory at the cross and showing them the
implications of the *sacramentum* of baptism, that military
oath after which no desertion is allowed but only participation in Christ's suffering. In this same room Christians must
have gathered many times to celebrate the eucharist, the
remembrance and representation of Christ's self-offering,
before they themselves went out to be offered in obedience
to God in their daily life and in their ultimate offering of
martyrdom.

Yet just behind this ancient house-church and still beneath the church of St. Clement is another room which
could tell many a tale.[2] When one enters one sees on each
side a bench of stone where during their meetings the consecrated members of the Mithras cult sat in the dark cellar
which now and then was suddenly lit up. In the middle
stands a sculpture of a young man slaughtering a bull. This

is Mithras, a god of light and of the sun, known in India
and especially in Persia. The most famous legend about
him tells how once he caught a bull, brought him into a
grove and slaughtered him. Then the miracle happened
that wherever the blood of the bull dripped down, grain
grew. Out of death came miraculously new life. If one
looks at the ceiling of that place of worship of the Mithras
mysteries beneath St. Clement's one sees a series of holes.
During the initiation and consecration ceremonies a bull
was slaughtered upstairs and the life-giving blood of the
victim dripped down through the holes on the "brethren,"
as the members of the Mithras cult called one another. This
must have been a ghastly sight. There is an account, by a
Christian eye-witness, of such a *taurobolium* in which the
worshipers were drenched with the blood of a bull; but I
will spare the reader this revolting scene.[3] Among those
who sat on the stone benches there were certainly Roman
legionaries, for the cult of Mithras was predominantly a
soldier's religion. In fact, it was mainly through the army
that this cult had been introduced into the West after the
military expeditions of Pompey in Asia Minor. The cult
never penetrated into the domain of Hellenism where it was
considered barbarous, but it was to be found wherever the
Roman army went, especially on the frontiers of the Roman
provinces where the legions were stationed. This is not astonishing, for Mithraism was exclusively a man's religion.
No women were admitted, and the whole emphasis lay on
the military virtues. The third of the seven stages which a
consecrated member could pass through after his initiation
was actually called *miles,* the soldier. To enter that stage
the initiated had to consecrate himself through a *sacramentum* to service in the legions of the *Deus invictus,* the
invincible god of the sun. There were rites of baptism and

holy meals which in their appearance and terminology had
so much similarity with Christian worship that this became
a scandal to the Church Fathers. They explained it as a
devilish imitation of the worship of the church. Tertullian
wrote, for instance, about Mithraism: "The devil baptizes
certain folk, his believers and faithful ones, promising re-
mission of sins after immersion. And if I still recollect
rightly, Mithras sets a mark on the forehead of his soldiers,
celebrates the oblation of bread, introduces a symbol of the
resurrection, and wins a crown under the sword. And what
are we to say of Satan restricting his high priest to one
marriage? The devil, too, has his virgins and his chaste
celibates" (*De praescr. haer.* XI). Even earlier Justin in-
cluded the following revealing aside in his description of
the eucharist: "This also the wicked demons in initiation
handed down as something to be done in the mysteries of
Mithras; for bread and a cup of water are brought out in
their secret rites of initiation, with certain invocations
which you either know or can learn" (*Apol.* 66). We no
longer know the sacramental words which were spoken in
such ceremonies, but in the Mithraeum of Aventin the following revealing inscription was found: "Thou hast saved
men by the pouring of eternal blood."

There was indeed some reason for anxiety among Christians, because from the end of the second century onwards
Mithraism claimed to be a universal religion, and rallied
forces with the cult of the emperor. In the third century
Rome became the headquarters of the Mithras cult, in which
the emperor was worshiped as *consubstantivum soli,* co-
essential with the sun. The struggle between Christianity
and paganism became more and more a struggle between
the militant church and the soldiers' religion of Mithras.

Towards the end of the fourth century the outcome of this conflict was clear. As a sign of it, at several places churches were built above the cellars where Mithras worship took place, and St. Clement's in Rome above the ancient house-church and the Mithraeum symbolizes this dramatic beginning of Western Christendom.

I.

Why is it that a Christian church stands today at St. Clement's and not a great temple of Mithras? Many reasons could be given. Probably the most profound, however, appears as soon as one compares the specific Christian concept of sacrifice with the nature and aim of sacrifices in the mystery religions and in fact in all other religions of this world. While maintaining sacrificial imagery and terminology, Christ and his apostles gave a radically new interpretation of the meaning of sacrifice.[4] It can be summed up in the following five statements which will be explained more fully: (1) The traditional function of the priest is abandoned; instead of offering sacrifices the priest is now himself to become the victim. (2) This new pattern laid down by Christ has to mark the whole life of the church, which has not in the first place a priestly function, but that of a victim. (3) The self-sacrifice of Christ's church is not restricted to a sacred place and time, nor is it offered in order to gain salvation, but it takes place in the midst of the everyday life of the world, and it is offered to thank God for the gift of salvation and to extend it unto the ends of the earth and of time. (4) In this sacrifice the combat with the powers and principalities reaches its climax and the church, like Christ, becomes a victorious victim. (5) In

order to lead and sustain the church in this victorious
sacrifice, Christ called ministers to be examples of victorious
victims.

1. In the New Testament church there was no place for
a regular priesthood, as priesthood was understood at that
time. True, "very many of the priests adhered to the Faith"
(Acts 6:7), but there is not a single indication that they
fulfilled a special role in the church. According to the
Gospels, Jesus himself never assumed the title "priest." He
claimed and was given many names: Messiah or Christ,
Shepherd, Judge, King, Lord, Son of man, Son of God. Yet
never did he call himself a priest and never did he give this
title to his disciples. He did not speak about his or our
priestly work, but about his suffering and the suffering of
his followers which is inevitably implied in the submission
to the will of the Father and in the work of the Servant.
The image of the Suffering Servant of the Lord which is
painted in the prophecies of the Second Isaiah must have
been increasingly in the mind of our Lord during the latter
part of his earthly ministry. He actually quoted the most
famous Servant Song (Isaiah 52:13–53:12) on the eve of the
crucifixion. Only twice did our Lord speak about his baptism, the initiation into his ministry, and both times he
related it to his cross (Mark 10:38; Luke 12:50). His ministry was to be fulfilled in and through self-sacrifice. Equally,
the apostle Paul never spoke about Christ as the priest, but
as the victim, the "passover lamb" that was once for all
sacrificed for us (Rom. 3:25; I Cor. 5:8). Only the author
of the letter to the Hebrews called Christ a priest, yet it is
just in this letter that the radically new interpretation of
the priest's function becomes most apparent: (a) as the
eternal high priest Christ sacrificed himself at the cross,

becoming both priest and victim; (*b*) in contrast to the continually repeated ceremonies of traditional sacrifices, this sacrifice was unique and unrepeatable; nevertheless it is perpetually effective and constantly operative. (*c*) This is so because Christ's self-sacrifice not only wiped out the sinful past of the human race but provided a new beginning for God's people living under a New Covenant. Therefore Christ's high-priesthood superseded all the existing sacrificial ritual by "his complete self-dedication in unreserved obedience to God his Father and in unlimited love and compassion towards men his brethren."[5]

Mithras offered the blood of a bull. In all religions, priests and believers offered something, some animal or even some human beings to God in their sacrifices. Christ, however, obeying God and loving men to the end, offered his own lifeblood.

2. This new concept of priesthood and sacrifice is normative for the church. Especially in Protestantism, the term "priesthood of all believers" has gained much popularity and is often used as the clue for the understanding of the task of the church and its members.[6] It must be noted, however, that this is not a typical New Testament concept. Neither Christ nor the evangelists ever used this term and it does not occur either in the letters of Paul and his disciples. Three times in the Book of Revelation (1:6; 5:10; 20:6) and once in I Peter (2:5, 9) the term "royal priesthood" occurs in direct or indirect quotations of two Old Testament passages (Exodus 19:6; Isaiah 61:6), but this certainly does not warrant the centrality given by most Protestants to this concept. As with regard to Christ, so also with regard to the church, the emphasis lies not on the term priest but on victim. Nobody likes this. To be a priest is something quite

respectable. To become a victim, however, hurts. Yet this is exactly our calling, as T. W. Manson has shown:

> The priesthood of all believers lies in the fact that each believer offers himself as a sacrifice according to the pattern laid down by Christ; and—what is equally essential—that all these individual offerings are taken up into the one perpetual offering made by the one eternal high-priest of the New Covenant.
>
> [Christians are now] permitted and enabled to share in the continuing high-priestly work of Christ by offering themselves in love and obedience to God and in love and service of men.[7]

While the members of the Mithras cult were onlookers at the sacrifices offered by the father-priest, the members of the *militia Christi* offer themselves as a living sacrifice. This is most clearly expressed in Romans 12:1[8] where Paul took up again the line of thought which he began in Romans 6 when speaking about our baptism into the cross, the death and resurrection of Christ. On the basis of this dramatic baptismal anticipation of, and initiation into, what has to be worked out in a daily dying and rising, Paul had already asked the Christians in Rome to present themselves to God and their members as weapons of righteousness. While there he used the verb "to present" with a military overtone, in Romans 12 he gave it the meaning in which it occurs several times in the Old Testament and where it designates the act of cultic offering: "I implore you by God's mercy to offer your very selves to him: a living sacrifice, dedicated and fit for his acceptance." This can only happen through "God's mercies," by which term Paul summed up the total history of salvation, especially all that Christ did for us when at the cross he became the victorious victim and when at baptism he let us share in his death and new life by the Spirit. As the objects of

God's mercy we are made "living," "holy," "blameless,"
"acceptable" and "well-pleasing," which in the Old Testament are all technical terms for describing the victim which
is fit to be sacrificed. Yet such a life, holiness and election
are not ends in themselves. They are given in order that the
church may be taken into Christ's sacrifice. In Romans 12:1
it is said that the baptized themselves bring their very selves
to the altar. In other texts this function is given to the
apostle. Ultimately, however, it is Christ himself who offers
his body, the church.[9]

3. Christ was not sacrificed in a holy place and on a holy
day, but outside the gates of Jerusalem and on the day before
the Sabbath. When he died "the curtain of the temple was
torn in two from top to bottom" (Matt. 27:51); the place
called the holy of holies was opened; all nations could now
enter, and the clearcut division between the sacred and the
secular was abolished. After this event the church is not
allowed to retire into a religious ghetto. Christ is not there.
He went out into the world to suffer there for all nations.
The writer of the letter to the Hebrews exhorts us: "Let
us then go to him outside the camp"; and in the same
context he tells us what kind of sacrifices are now expected
from us. "Through Jesus let us continually offer up to God
the sacrifices of praise, that is, the tributes of lips which
acknowledge his name, and never forget to show kindness
and to share what you have with others; for such are the
sacrifices which God approves" (13:13–16).

While those initiated into the sacrificial mysteries of
Mithras came together for their secret cults at set times and
places, the whole life of the militant church becomes a continuous worship and sacrifice. Also Christians assemble for
the sacrifice of praise, especially the eucharist, in which the

sacrificed Lord had promised to be present with his disciples
in a special way. However, Christian sacrifice is by no means
restricted to these assemblies and it is a dangerous one-
sidedness to speak of sacrifice mainly or exclusively in terms
of the eucharist, as happens so often among theologians. To
a great extent the apostle Paul used secular terms for describing what happens in gatherings for worship, while quite
often he used cultic and sacrificial terms for his own missionary work and for the witness and service of Christians
in the world. This is significant. Worship cannot be restricted to the sacrifice of praise for the salvation which
Christ gained for us. It includes also the sacrifice of labor
in missionary work and service so that the salvation which
Christ gained for *all* becomes effective. Moreover, while the
sacrifices in the Mithras cult were offered in order to gain
salvation for the initiates of this mystery religion, the militant church needs no more sacrifice for this purpose. Not to
gain salvation, but to thank God for it and to extend its
effectiveness, the militant church offers itself. For this purpose alone are the church and its ministers called to be spent,
to be used up in sacrifice.

4. Faced with this typically Christian sacrifice the powers
and principalities are powerless. The *passio,* the suffering of
self-sacrifice, is the most effective form of *actio,* of action
and combat. Nothing disarms the attacks of the powers
of death more thoroughly than this sacrifice. No wonder,
therefore, that there is an intimate link between the sacrificial and military terminology of the New Testament.

When it comes to the suffering for Christ's sake, the line
between the *militia Christi* and the *militia mundi* finally
becomes clear. In Romans 12:2 Paul mentions three steps
which are necessary in order that the continuous worship

of our life can become a living sacrifice: the first step is to take a firm stand in the ranks of the militant church. No more conformity with "the spirit of this age"[10] is allowed, for each one must now conform to the Christ-Victim. Yet with this non-conformity to the pattern of this present world (Rom. 12:2a) a second step has to be made: we have to be remolded (the original text says literally "metamorphosed") by a constant return to the new power and criteria of judgment which we received at baptism. The New English Bible translates: "Let your minds be remade and your whole nature thus transformed" (12:2b). Without this painful inner struggle, this agony of change, the outward combat cannot be fought. Only then are we ready for what the sacrifice according to the pattern of Christ really means from day to day in the workaday world: the obedience to God's will, and this no more in the form of conformity to a once-for-all, set law of God or to so-called Christian principles, but as the obedient response of the sons whose ethical imagination is alive and who can discern the will of their living Father (12:2c).

The intimate connection between sacrificial and military/athletic imagery is especially obvious in the letter to the Hebrews,[11] which is not a dry theological treatise about the priesthood of Christ, but a *mot d'ordre,* an encouragement to marching soldiers (cf. 12:12–13). With a few telling words the author points to the drama of salvation: Christ became man "so that through death he might break the power of him who had death at his command, that is, the devil; and might liberate those who, through fear of death, had all their lifetime been in servitude. . . ." Therefore he had to be made like these brothers of his in every way, so that he might be merciful and faithful as their high priest before God, to expiate the sins of the people. "For since he himself has passed through the test of suffering [later it is even said that "he learned obedience in the school of suffering,"(5:8)], he is able to help those who are meeting their test now" (2:14–18). Rightly Christ is therefore called our "pioneer" (2:10; 12:2) and the "forerunner" (6:20). This picture of the stadium where an *agōn*,[12] a race, has to be won and a combat fought, dominates the whole letter. Having spoken about the champions of faith in the old covenant (chap. 11) the author considers these champions as the spectators for the *agōn* of the militant church, and he says: "With all these witnesses to faith around us like a cloud, we must throw off every encumbrance, every sin to which we cling, and run with resolution the race for which we are entered, our eyes fixed on Jesus, on whom faith depends from start to finish: Jesus who, for the sake of the joy that lay ahead of him, endured the cross, making light of its disgrace, and has taken his seat at the right hand of the throne of God" (12:1–2). This was not meant as a harmless encouragement in an athletic contest, but as the preface to martyrdom (12:3–4).

5. The champions of faith of the old covenant may now be spectators of the struggle and agony of the militant church, but not so the ordained ministers! Missionaries, pastors, bishops, teachers and all the other ministers have been ordained to be spent in service. The verb "to be spent" (*spendomai*) is a biblical term which comes straight from the world of sacrifice and means "to be poured out as a libation, a drink offering." Paul used it in this sense in Philippians 2:17 which reads in the literal translation: "If I am poured out as a libation upon that sacrifice which is the offering up of your faith, I am glad of it." This of course does not mean that each minister should be so busy

that before long he soon becomes ill through overwork and dies of a heart attack. Like Christ's suffering, the ministerial suffering is not over-busyness but first of all the agony of prayer and intercession, the carrying of the burden of others. If one studies the New Testament evidence about the apostles and their collaborators one soon discovers that to be a minister of the church does not mean to have a religious profession, to fulfil a much-honored position in society as did the priests in Israel and the priests of all religions. The call to be a minister is first of all a call to labor[13] in the double sense of this word: labor as hard and painful work and labor as the sufferings of childbirth. "I am in travail with you over again until you take the shape of Christ," wrote Paul to the Galatians (4:19) when they were in danger of falling out of the domain of God's grace.

In a careful study Antony T. Hanson has shown that the apostle Paul used exactly the same terms for describing the work of apostles and their collaborators as he used for describing the work and sacrifice of Christ.[14] The life of the ministers thus reproduces in the church the life of Christ, the purpose being that the church as a whole should live out Christ's atoning life in the world. While the priests of mystery religions are set apart from and above the members of the cult, have secret knowledge of mysteries and fulfil functions which no one else may fulfil, the ministers of the church have no such exclusive state, knowledge and task: nothing is said of them which could not be said of the church as a whole. It is not they alone who celebrate the eucharist, but they lead the church in its celebration of the eucharist. It is not they alone who witness to the gospel, but they strengthen the church for its witness and service. In the churches in Asia and Africa the first converts are often called to be the ministers because they were the pioneers

of faith. So in the New Testament the ministers' distinctive
quality was that they were pioneers of a pioneering church,
and this meant pioneering in suffering for the church so
that the whole church might be drawn into the sacrifice for
the world.

II.

This emphasis on sacrifice and especially on the suffering
of pioneer ministers is utterly irrelevant in times when the
church dominates the world, as was often the case in the
so-called Christian West. Sacrificial terminology is also not
easily understandable wherever the church has settled down
in various religious groupings within the pluriform society
of areas with a high standard of living. Yet perhaps we have
become too much enslaved to a shallow and easy relevance.
We may have to seem irrelevant in our thoughts and actions for a long time in order that our life may become
again relevant to the gospel and the deepest needs of this
world. The New Testament concept of life as a living sacrifice
is not valid only for small minority churches living in a
hostile and consciously non-Christian environment. One
must admit, however, that during the last centuries of Western church history, especially in Protestant piety, the New
Testament concept of sacrifice played only a minor role. It
paid to be a Christian, only seldom did it pain, and the
ministers of the church received so many honors and worldly
securities that they could scarcely become pioneers in sacrificial living.[15]

Nevertheless, there are indications that the tide is changing. This may be the result of the fact that almost everywhere the church is making the sobering discovery that it
is increasingly becoming a minority living as a world-wide

Christian diaspora in the midst of a consciously or unconsciously non-Christian world.[16] It may also be caused by
the fact that Western Christians are now more ready to listen
to what members of the small minority churches in Asia
and Africa have to say, where the suffering for Christ's sake
never became an archaic form of speech. The rediscovery of
sacrifice is also intimately linked with the experience of the
churches who lived under persecution in the East and the
West. During the earthquake of the last world war many
saw the deep relevance of what on the surface still seems to
be irrelevant for the everyday life of twentieth-century laymen and ministers in the West.

One of the most precious documents of this rediscovery
is the, alas, too little known study on "The human experience of sacrifice"[17] written in captivity by Georges Gusdorf,
a French Protestant philosopher. Using Gabriel Marcel's
concepts of "being" and "having" (*être* and *avoir*) Gusdorf
showed: (*a*) that man always tends to possess his environment, but that these possessions threaten his being (in such
a predicament man found a possible but unsatisfactory way
of life by constantly exchanging his possessions); (*b*) that
from the beginning man searched for another way of life,
the way of sacrifice, but failed to follow it through to the
end; and (*c*) that Christ went the adventurous way of self-
sacrifice, calling us to join him now on this way.

a) No human being can live alone, isolated from the
things and persons of his environment. No man is sufficient
unto himself. In order to live, the "being" must take possession of its environment. The "being" continually tends
to the "having." But to have, to possess something or somebody, degrades and kills the object and enslaves the subject.
No true communication is established. The being is thus

continually threatened by the having. In this predicament
man has found a way of life, through the constant exchange
of possessions and ideas. Reciprocity and partnership charac-
terize each human society, both the most primitive society
and such a highly complicated structure as the modern
American business society. One word evokes the other to
become a dialogue, and one action evokes the other to become a continuous transaction. In such a universe of exchange, where everything is ordered according to a written
or unwritten social contract, human life becomes possible,
but man is then still man in slavery, potential man rather
than a mature human being. In such a world of exchange
disinterested gifts point already to another way of life. They
become an anticipation of sacrifice. Yet even gifts evoke an
answer, be it only the answer of thankfulness or irritation
(Emerson remarked rightly that "we do not quite forgive a
giver").

   b) There is, however, another form of communication
with the material and spiritual realities of this world: the
way of sacrifice, which frees and matures man. Gusdorf
showed how, from the beginning, man has tried to travel
this way, not only in his religious practices, but also in his
search for a human ethic. Sacrifice is also a sort of exchange
and gift. It is the offering of the old and limited being
which man is now, in order to become receptive for a new
and fuller being which breaks with the established order.
Each sacrifice is thus an adventure filled with surprises. It
means walking out of a small and secure place into a large
space. It is a liberation from routine and gives a new beginning. The old being which is imprisoned and suffocated by
its possessions can escape into a new being, if it is ready to
pay the price of sacrifice. Yet exactly at this point the human
attempt to travel the way of sacrifice has usually stopped

half-way. Throughout human history one sees individual persons, groups and whole nations going the initial stage of the way of sacrifice, offering something of their possessions or even sacrificing other human beings in order to attain a new being. Yet on the way of sacrifice one soon discovers that it is not enough to sacrifice something or somebody else. Inevitably the way leads to the adventure of self-sacrifice. During the exceptional times of war men were ready to sacrifice themselves for their country and the liberty to be gained. Yet in normal life man shies away from such self-sacrifice, especially when it does not demand dying heroically with fellowmen traveling the same way, but when it implies a daily dying and rising, a long sacrificial life in the midst of a universe of exchange. Faced with this more difficult stage on the way of sacrifice almost no one dares to go further. Most cling to their old being. Sacrifice then degenerates into exchange: something or somebody else is offered in order to preserve the old self. Part is given in order to safeguard the whole.

c) One man, however, went the way of sacrifice to the end: Jesus Christ. He was not constrained by outer circumstances—he could have asked God for legions of angels to fight for him! Being the Son of God and without sin he had no need to exchange an old being for a new being or to gain salvation. Out of free will he obeyed God and loved man to the end and thus gained salvation for all. He now calls us to follow him on this way of self-sacrifice. He is ready to accept our half-hearted and imperfect sacrifices, which always degenerate into exchange, and to take them into his perfect sacrifice. Yet he demands that those who follow him reject the offering of a life other than their own. Knowing his sacrifice for their salvation, they need no more safeguard their old being, but can lose it in thankfulness to God and while being spent for the world. All those who dare to go this adventurous way in following Christ are being changed. They live no more under the tyranny of "the ethics of the must" where everything is fixed by set laws and principles. They live according to "the ethics of sacrifice," which acts by innovation, by ethical imagination. They dare to do the unusual, which often may seem to be the immoral and godless, precisely because they discern Christ suffering outside the religious camp in the midst of the secular world.

All this is not modern existentialist philosophy, as some might suspect. It is a meditation on the words of our Lord who said that "if anyone wishes to be a follower of mine, he must leave self behind. Whoever cares for his own safety is lost; but if a man will let himself be lost for my sake, he will find his true self" (Matt. 16:24f.).

In the light of this meditation about sacrifice, one would now have to examine the present life of the church, its members and its ministers. Are we on the way of sacrifice, on that typically Christian way to victory?

What about the movement for Christian stewardship which originated in the United States and now spreads all over the world? Is this an indication that our generation begins to understand what sacrifice according to Christ's pattern means? Does the offering of some time, talents and money for God's work in and through organized church activities help Christians to see that *all* their time, talents and possessions, in fact their very being, are claimed by God in order to be spent in the servant church in and for the world? Or is the stewardship movement a new method of godless powers and principalities which deceive Christians with the illusion that by giving part of one's time, talents and money to a religious institution one may keep

the whole of the old sinful life and self? There are many
examples which show that the stewardship movement can
indeed be both: a first step on the way of sacrifice and a
new method of the devil.

What about the prevalent Christian ethic and way of life?
Is it an "ethic of the must" or an "ethic of sacrifice"? Is it a
moralistic preservation of the *status quo* or the adventure
of renewal and liberation? Many church leaders were deeply
shocked when at the last Assembly of the World Council of
Churches an Indian Christian lawyer spoke in the following
terms about his Christian lawyer's vocation: "The lawyer's
role is to be an advocate of the law breaker. . . . He is not
the advocate of God or the 'good' against man. . . . Hence
there exists no Christian basis whatsoever for any lawyer
to wash his hands of 'dirty cases.' "[18] In the same address it
was said that Christians will necessarily get dirty hands and
that therefore an ethic which helps to distinguish the legiti-
mate from the illegitimate compromise is overdue. This does
not sound very moral, but it certainly is Christian. We are
the church of One who knew the hard facts of life. He lived
as a craftsman in a business world where corruption played
a big role. In an occupied country he associated with cen-
turions of the colonial army, with tax-gatherers, fishermen
and prostitutes, accepting their poor efforts to understand
him and work with him, while at the same time he fought
the respectable priests and lawyers of God's law who honestly sought to know and do God's will. As the church of
this Christ, we must become the focus of the sufferings in
our time. Instead of defending God against doubts and
attacks, the militant church is called to open its heart and
fellowship to the agony of the world, continuously struggling
in intercession while being spent in service.

Finally, what about the securities of our creeds? Do we

consider them as possessions and use them in order to assert
ourselves and our special denominations and traditions?
Or are we living the adventure of faith which in the strength
of the gospel and its assurance dares to give up old ties and
familiar security in order to be reborn into a fuller community and a deeper understanding of the truth of Christ?
The continuation of church divisions indicates that in this
respect we do not walk in the way of sacrifice. Yet, there is
an even greater sacrifice asked from us today with regard to
the security offered by our creeds. Instead of considering
such security as our possession and so asserting our religious
superiority above poor atheist and non-religious man, we
must learn again the adventure of faith. In the strength of
the gospel we must dare to suffer even with the deepest
suffering of our time, the sense of God-forsakenness, i.e., the
apparent silence, ambiguity and absence of God. Often in
solidarity with those who doubt and those who can no more
believe, we must wait until together we recognize the presence of God. Having thus sacrificed the security offered by
our creeds we may then suddenly meet there with the "out-
siders," the living Christ who still bears outside the camp
the agony of the world as the Suffering Servant and the
Victorious Victim.

5

DISARMING JOY

Around the year A.D. 50 the inhabitants of the prison in Philippi must have had a memorable night. The day before there had been a tumult in the city. A Jewish tentmaker with strange powers of healing had released a slave-girl from her demon. This very much displeased the owner of the girl, because he earned a great deal of money by her prophecies through ventriloquism. He organized a mob to support his denunciation and succeeded in having the Jewish tentmaker and his colleagues severely flogged and then securely locked up in prison. That seemed the end of it. The only result one could foresee was a sleepless night for the new prisoners (for Roman flogging was no minor thing) and perhaps some groaning from the direction of their cell. Yet at midnight all the prisoners awoke, and what they heard were not groans, but hymns of praise. The prison had become a temple, a place for offering thanks and making shouts of praise, instead of lamentation and cursing. Paul and Silas—for they were the singing prisoners in Philippi—became the predecessors of a whole army of Christian prisoners who, in the course of church history, have sung praises in prison, up to that French Christian who during the Second World War wrote in a concentration camp a study about the laughter of God.[1] Yet there were even more astonishing things to happen during that memorable night in Philippi, if we can credit Luke's account.[2] A violent earthquake burst the prison doors open and all the prisoners could have escaped.

Assuming that this had indeed happened, the jailer attempted to commit suicide, but Paul intervened just in time. The end of the story is well known. First there was the classic missionary dialogue: the non-Christian, astonished by the attitudes and deeds of the Christians and discerning a divine mystery in and behind their lives, asked: "What must I do to be saved?" The Christians answered: "Put your trust in the Lord Jesus, and you will be saved, you and your household." Then followed baptism. Those who had become prisoners of war[3] in the battle of faith had not ceased to struggle for their mission of peace. The Church Fathers later called the prisons *castra Dei,* "war camps of God." Prisons were places for the struggle of intercession, meditation and thanksgiving, and what happened as a result of this in Philippi has happened ever since: the jailers joined the army of Christ. When the morning of that memorable night came we find the jailer of Philippi at table with his former prisoners, and he "rejoiced with his whole household in his new-found faith in God."

"He rejoiced in his faith." This is a typical New Testament expression. The militant church is a joyous company. However, to be realistic one had better say that it should be a joyous company, for we must acknowledge that, generally speaking, Christians do not strike observers as particularly joyous people in their worship and daily life. On the contrary! Even in the first centuries of church history the enemies of the church pointed to the fact that Christians knew no humor and enjoyment, that they tended to see only the dark, grave and otherworldly side of things, and that, contrary to this, the Greek philosophers knew how to smile and laugh and had a sense of humor, wit and gaiety. This classic charge against Christians, which has been voiced throughout the centuries until today, is now being rejected by modern Christian writers. Many articles and booklets have recently appeared, especially in German, with titles such as "The virtue of gaiety," "Gay spirituality," "About the humor of Christians." The famous church historian Hans von Campenhausen has now critically examined both the non-Christian charge and the modern popular Christian apology[4] and the following are some of his observations.

In the New Testament and the writings of the Church Fathers one finds indeed little or no humor. Once or twice the apostle Paul may have told some rather crude jokes (Gal. 5:12), in order to ridicule his opponents. In the same polemic way jokes are used by Tertullian, Jerome and other Church Fathers, but we would scarcely want to call this a particularly Christian kind of humor. In isolated places in their writings some Church Fathers advise the Christians not to be gloomy because the Christian life is a divine children's play, "a smile supported by patience" (Clement of Alexandria). Yet such a sorrowful joy, such sophisticated knowledge that our life is a mixture of comedy and tragedy, of laughter and weeping, of jest and gravity is not a specifically Christian trait of character either. It has its origin in Socrates rather than in Christ.

Humor and wit are thus not special Christian characteristics. It would be wrong, however, to maintain that Christian faith is the end of humor. It is true that in early monasticism laughter was considered irreverent and that in his famous rule St. Benedict admonished the monks to be "not easily and quickly moved by laughter" and to speak "quietly and without laughter" (chap. vii). Yet it is precisely in early monasticism that humor also broke through in the Christian church. In the medieval Easter liturgies laughter even received a liturgical place. After the fasting, sorrow and austerity of the weeks before Easter, laughter had to be learned again, and this happened during the liturgy of the first or second Easter day when the priest told funny stories in his sermon and the whole congregation burst out laughing. The medieval cathedrals were indeed not only places of worship in awe, but also places of gay worship. Many of the cathedrals' sculptures, not only the famous "laughing angel" of Bamberg, evoke our smile and laughter.[5] Ever since the Middle Ages there has been an uninterrupted series of Christians who became well-known also because of their sense of humor, for instance, men like Martin Luther and Karl Barth.[6]

If one explores the humor of a Luther or a Barth, one soon discovers that its origin is not just a natural disposition (Luther was actually inclined to melancholy) nor the Socratic view of life; it comes, rather, from their faith in Jesus Christ. It is an expression of the typically Christian joy. This joy certainly belongs to the heart of Christian faith. The apostle Paul who badly lacked humor was joyous in prison and did not cease to exhort Christians to be joyful. The classical Greek terms for gladness such as *eudaimonia, hēdonē,* and *hilarotes* occur seldom or never in the New Testament, but the terms "joy," "rejoice," "glad confidence" abound.[7] In fact there is probably no other book in the world where the word "joy" occurs so often.

I.

Christian joy does not on the surface seem to have much relationship with the military imagery of the New Testament. Nevertheless it is good to conclude this series of lectures on the militant church by highlighting the New Testament concept of joy,[8] and this for two reasons: first, because throughout the centuries it has been a particular temptation of the militant church to become so engrossed with its battle of faith that it loses the joy of faith; second, because there is a deep inner relationship between the combat of the militant church and the joy which breaks through in Christian life. On each of the four points dealt with in these lectures— (1) baptism, (2) mission, (3) equipment and (4) suffering—Christians are surprised by joy. No wonder therefore that New Testament writers saw also an intimate connection between (5) the work of ordained ministers and the joy of the church.

1. When the jailer of Philippi and his family had been baptized, "he rejoiced with his whole household in his new-found faith in God." The same connection between baptism and joy is reported earlier in Acts (8:39), when Philip the evangelist met an African eunuch on the road from Jerusalem to Gaza and baptized him according to his wish. The eunuch went his way with joy—a promising beginning to African church history. Where uncritically imported Western forms of worship do not yet, or no longer cripple the worship of the church one can even now hear shouts of joy at baptismal services in Africa. New names are given at these feasts, names such as "The one who was made glad" or "God is joy."[9]

Why this joy? Among the converts of the young churches in Asia and Africa the total event of baptism is experienced as a tremendous liberation, even as it was in the early church. Christ is victor over powers and principalities, and in baptism he takes the converts from the defeated army into his victorious company. While the military terminology shows mainly the antagonistic elements of the threefold event of baptism, the joy adds the victorious element, the resurrection aspect: (*a*) In the act of the baptismal renuncia-

tion of the devil the converts take sides in the cosmic struggle and say "no" to their old life and to the powers which
dominated it. The converts can do so with confident joy because they know that the cosmic victory has been won. They
need no more take the powers and principalities in dead
seriousness. They know about God's laughter at all those
who want to fight him and they may even join in God's
ironic laughter.[10] (b) In the act of baptismal incorporation
the converts confess their faith and thus take their military
oath. They can do so confidently because the blood of Christ
the victim has not only washed away their sinful past but
also gives them and the whole world a new beginning, the
immersion in the baptismal water being a sign and seal for
both. Instead of having to boast of their own works and
religious achievements the converts can now boast of the
fact that Christ the victim became victor.[11] (c) In the act of
baptismal ordination God equips and authorizes the converts for joining his mission of peace. Yet, by the same act,
he permits them to join the feast of the eucharist. In early
Christian worship these eucharistic meals were characterized
by rejoicing because the whole emphasis lay on the presence
of the victorious Christ who was with his disciples at the
Easter meals, who is now present with his militant church
on earth and who in the coming kingdom will sit with his
total church at the marriage banquet.[12]

2. The joy at baptism which reflects the light of resurrection permeates also the whole mission of peace. Recent
scholarship has shown that the great command at the end
of the Gospel of Matthew is part of a coronation hymn.[13]
The ancient oriental ceremony of the enthronement of a
king fell into three parts: first, the elevation of the new
king, which in Matthew 28 is expressed by Christ's words:

"Full authority in heaven and on earth has been committed to me"; second, the presentation of the king, which was accompanied by the acclamation and proclamation of his kingship; in the case of the enthronement of Christ this acclamation and proclamation takes the form of the worship and mission of the church; and, third, the act of enthronement of which at the end of Matthew only Christ's speech from the throne is recorded, that greatest promise ever given: "Be assured, I am with you always, to the end of time." The mission of the militant church thus does not stand alone. It is the counterpart to the acclamation of the worshiping church. Its origin is not first of all the obedience to a command which an officer has given and which must therefore be obeyed, but it is overflowing joy. This becomes most apparent in the Easter hymns of the Orthodox church; these are the most glorious documents of Christian joy.[14] At midnight on Easter eve the Orthodox worship begins with the first hymn:

> Day of Resurrection,
> Let us shine forth in glory, O nations,
> Pascha, Pascha of the Lord.
> For Christ our God has led us from death unto life
> and from earth to heaven,
> us who sing the hymn of victory!

Yet this joy overflows. It is meant not just for the church, but for all nations, for the total creation. One of the last hymns therefore exhorts the worshipers to go and witness:

> Do not stay here in adoration, you women!
> Run as witnesses of the glad tidings.
> Accept from us the message of joy,
> The news of Christ's resurrection!
> Shout, rejoice and dance, Jerusalem:
> You saw Christ, the King!

The mission means not only to tell the glad news, it means also to live it. The Doxastikon at the end of the Easter liturgy is therefore an appeal for reconciliation, for living the mission of peace:

> Day of Resurrection!
> Let us be glorious in splendour
> for the festival,
> and let us embrace one another.
> Let us say "Brethren" to those who hate us
> and in the resurrection let us forgive all things.
> And so let us shout:
> Christ has risen from the dead,
> by death he overcame death,
> and to those in the tombs
> He gave life.

These hymns show that neither worship nor mission are ends in themselves, but both are parts in the event of Christ's enthronement: He became the victorious King at his cross and resurrection; now, in the worship and mission of his church, he is manifesting his kingship; and both worship and mission point to the time when he will be revealed to all as the King of kings in his full glory. Looking back and forward to this King, knowing that he is present in worship and that he precedes[15] those whom he calls into his mission, the militant church can go forward with confidence in the struggle for peace.

3. Joy is also the most precious part of the equipment for gracious service. "God loves a cheerful giver" (II Cor. 9:7). Joy disarms powers and principalities no less than sacrifice does. Yet even more than the total spiritual armor and all *charismata* joy is a mysterious thing which we can never own and which nevertheless becomes a continuing gift. We

cannot make it. Self-made and self-conscious joy is ugly. To keep smiling while the heart remains indifferent or resentful is hypocrisy. The apostle Paul therefore called joy a fruit and not a work (Gal. 5:22). This harvest of the Spirit ripens only among those who accept the spiritual armor from God and use it for the God-given purpose.

The mystery of Christian joy lies in the fact that in this harvest of the Spirit the future glory and bliss of God's kingdom already breaks through in the present time. The pledge of the Spirit realizes the content of Christian hope even when this hope is not yet fulfilled. This is most clearly seen in the daring paradoxes Paul uses in II Corinthians 6:4ff. to describe his apostleship: ". . . in our sorrows we have always cause for joy; poor ourselves, we bring wealth to many; penniless, we own the world." Only one who lives in this world by the powers of the oncoming world can speak in such a way. The constant temptation of Christians, however, is either to escape this world or to live in this world by those powers which still hold it in their grip. Therefore, Paul did not tire of exhorting the congregations: "Let hope keep you joyful" (Rom. 12:12). This is not an appeal to keep smiling but to hold fast to Christian hope and to live according to this hope in everyday life.[16]

This kind of joy characterizes the spirituality of the militant church. The true objectivity (*Sachlichkeit*) and true humanity mentioned earlier would degenerate into cold and shallow this-worldliness without the mystery of joy. Joy is like the sun which breaks through fog and suddenly sheds warm light on the things and people of this world. This joy also marks the ministry of the militant church. It gives belonging to Christ's company its spontaneous *rayonnement,* its radiant power and abundance. This abundant joy operates in love. For the apostle Paul joy had indeed a central

ethical connotation, and joy was for him intimately connected with love.

4. The mystery of Christian joy has throughout the centuries been most astonishing when Christians were surprised
by joy in the midst of their suffering for Christ's sake.[17] In
the Hellenistic mystery religions the state of happiness came
after the suffering, but Christian joy breaks through in the
midst of suffering. In the New Testament the term joy is in
fact most often used in the context of suffering. How can
this paradox be explained? Unlike the egocentric *eudaimonia*
of the mystery religions the Christian *chara* is always a "joy
in the Lord." It comes from Christ's presence and the believer's participation in the life of the Lord, not from a
cultic experience of happiness. It is a joy in view of the
coming reconciliation of all nations and the total universe
and not just a presently experienced individual exaltation,
as was the case in the mystery religions on the day of the
Hilaria after the day of Sanguis. It is a joy working in love
and not a hedonistically savored moment of happiness. Even
today Christ is present not only as the risen Lord, but also
as the suffering and crucified servant. Whenever someone
is called to suffer with Christ this is therefore a proof that
he is a living member of Christ's Body and that the powers
of resurrection are also operative in him. The joy in suffering
is thus an anticipation of the joy of resurrection. Only by
following the Lord in his self-offering can we follow him in
his victory and glory. Therefore Paul dared to call the suffering of the Philippians a special grace (Phil. 1:29). Therefore the Thessalonians who received the good news with
great joy, despite the grave sufferings it caused them, became a model for all believers (I Thess. 1:6f.). Christians can
even boast of their sufferings (Rom. 5:3), because sufferings

for Christ's sake and glory are not opposed to the logic of faith, but the one leads to the other: "We are God's heirs and Christ's fellow heirs, if we share his sufferings now in order to share his splendour hereafter" (Rom. 8:17). "As Christ's cup of suffering overflows, and we suffer with him, so also through Christ our consolation overflows" (II Cor. 1:5).

Without this joy in the Lord Christian self-offering soon becomes deadly serious and self-conscious and thus loses its Christian flavor. It is not we who suffer for the Lord and the world, it is he who lets us participate in the adventure of his self-sacrifice.

5. "We are not lording over your faith, but we work with you for your joy." This is the literal translation of what Paul wrote to the Corinthians (II Cor. 1:24), and it would be a good thing if all ministers of the church could honestly say the same about their work. The study of the Pauline texts in which joy is linked with the work of ministers confirms what was said in the earlier chapters about the ministers of the militant church.[18]

The ministers share in the joy of the church, yet they do not work for their own enjoyment. In fact Paul experienced very little natural happiness in his work. On the contrary, it became for him, and sometimes for the churches he served, an occasion of distress and worry. Of course, Christian joy is the end of the deadly worrying to which the world is submitted. Yet, if worries, hurts and miseries are "borne in God's way," worry ceases to be the opposite of joy but actually engenders joy (II Cor. 2:1–7; 7:8–11). Worry then becomes sympathy, which means literally "suffering together with." Indeed, in Paul's lifework joy first of all broke through in his apostolic sufferings. Not the apostolic work

in itself, but the sacrificial way of doing this work, became
for Paul a reason for exaltation, because this conformity to
the pattern of Christ's sacrifice gave him the joyous assurance
that he was really Christ's minister to the church. Therefore he rejoiced in the expectation of his martyrdom (Phil.
2:17f.). This is also the context of that astonishing statement
made in the letter to the Colossians: "It is now my happiness
to suffer for you. This is my way of helping to complete, in
my poor human flesh, the full tale of Christ's afflictions still
to be endured, for the sake of his body which is the church"
(1:24). The fruit of such sacrifice is the inward and outward
growth of the church, and this growth became another
source of joy for Paul. The joy of the church in Thessa-
lonica, despite its grave sufferings, became not only a model
for all Christians but also Paul's hope, joy or crown. "It is
you who are indeed our glory and our joy" (I. 2:19f.). This
sometimes led Paul to joyous pride in Christ's work through
him (Phil. 2:16), but more often to that joyous thanksgiving
(I Thess. 3:9f.) which is the basic attitude of a true minister.

II.

This mystery of joy which transcends both human sad-
ness and gaiety and which can also be given to those who
have little sense of humor belongs essentially to the struggle
of the militant church. At the end of his life Cardinal
Suhard, who was the great spiritual leader under whom the
French Roman Catholic church became again the militant
church in pagan French society, said something which illustrates this in a striking way: The one who witnesses to the
gospel is called not to be a propagandist but "to create a
mystery" (*de faire mystère*) by living and acting in the midst
of the world in such a way that this life cannot be ex-

plained, unless it be explained on the basis of the reality of God.[19] This mysterious and indefinable something must have radiated from the life of the early Christians, that kind of love, peace, joy and hope which evoked amazed or irritated questions (I Peter 3:17).

We know this mystery. It is Christ's presence through which the powers of the coming kingdom are already operative now. Not what *we* do or are, but our communion with *him* creates the mystery. It is participation in his mission, receiving his armor and joining his suffering which lead to the amazing joy in the Lord.

At the end of this book we can therefore sum up our task as the militant church in this one thing which is needed: to discern the presence of Christ in order to work and suffer with him. Where is Christ present today? Certainly in the proclamation of the good news and in the celebration of the eucharist. Not to hold fast to this great Reformation rediscovery would mean to despise God's assurance. Yet to say these two things only means to belittle God's promises. According to Matthew, Christ said that the whole world of history is nothing but "the birth-pangs of the new age" (Matt. 24:8). Paul wrote about the fact that "the whole created universe groans in all its parts as if in the pangs of childbirth" (Rom. 8:22); and in the letters to the Ephesians and Colossians we are given a glimpse of the cosmic dimensions of Christ's death and victory. This opens up perspectives about which the Greek Fathers knew much but which, for centuries, have scarcely been seen in the Western church. The agony of the world is not an illness leading to death, and its longings, revolutions and innovations are not in vain. It would be tempting to write here about that great new reformation discovery of our time which cuts across all confessional boundaries: the grasp of God's redemptive action in and through world history. One would have to mention the amazing letters of Christoph Blumhardt written to his son-in-law in China, where at the end of the nineteenth and the beginning of the twentieth century he foresaw the coming Asian revolution and welcomed it as God's act of judgment, justice and liberation.[20] These letters would have to be compared with the writings of the Indian sociologist M. M. Thomas, who says that "the Asian revolution can be interpreted both as a direct and indirect impact of Jesus Christ on Asia."[21] The view of world history developed by the controversial Jesuit father and palaeontologist Pierre Teilhard de Chardin, the *Letters and Papers from Prison* by Dietrich Bonhoeffer, the interpretation of the present technological revolution by the British scientist John Wren-Lewis, the evaluation of the Western social and economic developments by the German sociologist Dietrich von Oppen and the British economist Denis Mumby, as well as the discussions about prophecy in the present-day political East-West tension among the leading personalities of the Prague Peace Conference, would have to be mentioned.[22] These are only a few voices in the contemporary search for discerning the action of the triune God in world history and of Christ's presence in the midst of secular events. They are quite unequal in importance and chosen almost at random. Many of these voices may be very onesided or even heretical, but there is no doubt that our generation stands here at the edge of a great reformation discovery which means hope for the world and is therefore the source of abundant joy. It is good that the World Council of Churches has decided to focus its main study on this theme.[23] If this study is carried through not only by academic theologians but by the whole militant church, especially by those of its members who gain their knowledge of God (theology) in and through a discerning involvement in the changing power structures of this world, we may discover that it is true what a French priest wrote: "If we could see life with the eyes of God, we would see that nothing is profane in the world, but that, on the contrary, everything participates in the construction of God's kingdom. To have faith means, therefore, not only to lift up our eyes to God and contemplate him, it means also to look at this earth, but to do it with the eyes of Christ. . . . If we knew how to listen to God, if we knew how really to see life, all life would become prayer. For all life proceeds in God's sight and nothing must be lived without being offered up freely to him."[24] These are words of one who daily lives and works with the dock workers in the port of Le Havre, the Abbé Michel Quoist, who in his prayers and meditations has indeed gone a long way in discerning Christ's presence in the hard facts of life in the French proletariat. Unless the militant church learns to pray in this way, discerning the cosmic dimensions of Christ's sacrifice and victory and thus gaining hope for the whole world and great joy, its combat remains sterile. In the hymns of the Easter liturgy of the Orthodox church the whole cosmos is called upon to join in worship.

> Rejoice, you heavens, worthily,
> Earth, you sing too!
> The whole cosmos, shout with joy,
> the cosmos visible and invisible!
> Christ is risen,
> He the joy of ages.

In order that this may happen, that everyone and everything will be drawn into this cosmic liturgy, the militant church worships and struggles now on earth.

CHAPTER 1

¹ The ancient Christian baptistry of Jalyssos near the monastery Philerimos on Rhodes dates from the fifth or sixth century. It was excavated in 1947-49 by Mr. A. C. Orlandos. Cf. his article on "Les Baptistères du Dodécanèse" in *Actes due Vᵉ Congrès International d'Archéologie Chrétienne*, Aix-en-Provence, September, 1954 (Rome/Paris, 1957), pp. 199-211. Baptismal fonts in the form of the cross were not uncommon. A.C. Orlandos says about these fonts in the Dodecanese that "they had different forms, among which the form of the cross was the most commonly used" (p. 207). For a ground plan of the baptistry of Jalyssos see *op. cit.*, p. 201. Photographs of other baptismal fonts in the form of a cross can be found on pp. 194, 206, and in F. van der Meer and Christine Mohrmann, *Atlas of the Early Christian World* (London, 1958), illustration No. 408.

² The main texts are Rom. 8:38 f.; I Cor. 2:8; 15:24-26; Eph. 1:20 f.; 2:1 f.; 3:10; 6:12 and Col. 1:16; 2:15. Cf. H. Berkhof, *Christus en de Machten* (Nijkerk, 1953); G. B. Caird, *Principalities and Powers: A study in Pauline Theology*, (Oxford, 1956); Heinrich Schlier, *Mächte und Gewalten im Neuen Testament* (Freiburg, 1958).

³ See, e.g., the *Christus militans* relief in the baptistry of the Orthodox in Ravenna, from about the year 450, and the Christ mosaic in the chapel of the archbishop of Ravenna, from about the year 500. Reproductions of both in Ethelbert Stauffer, *Die Theologie des Neuen Testaments* (4th ed.; Gütersloh, 1948), illustrations Nos. 69 and 71.

⁴ Like the passages about the powers and principalities, so also the image of Christ the Victor over powers and principalities was for centuries half forgotten. This has changed since the book of Gustav Aulén, *Christus Victor* (London, 1931). E. Stauffer, *op. cit.* (English edition; London, 1955) has laid much emphasis on the "antagonistic interpretation" of the New Testament. A detailed biblical study of this subject is Ragnar Leivestad, *Christ the Conqueror; Ideas of conflict and victory in the New Testament* (London, 1954).

⁵ This liturgy is contained in the *traditio apostolica* by Hippolytus, a church order in Rome which dates back to the third century. Sanctus Hippolytus, *Treatise on the Apostolic Tradition* (London, 1937), pp. 33-38. A short description of the liturgy will be found in Lukas Vischer, *Ye Are Baptized* (Geneva, 1961), pp. 8-10.

⁶ The Greek term *hopla* which is used here meant originally "tools," "implements," and in a more special way "weapons." Only this last meaning occurs in the New Testament. Unfortunately both the Revised Standard Version and the New English Bible have used in Rom. 6:13 the general and not the specific meaning, which according to G. Kittel (ed.), *Theologisches Wörterbuch zum Neuen Testament* (*T.W.z.N.T.*), V, 293 f. (Oepke) is the only possible translation. The term occurs once in the literal sense in John 18:3 and five times in a figurative way in Paul's letters. Rom. 6:13 and 13:12 show that the struggle of the *militia Christi* is the task of all baptized, while in II Cor. 6:7 and 10:4 Paul speaks about his own particular missionary struggle, for which he needs "the weapons of righteousness." The verb "to arm" (*hoplizesthai*) occurs only once in the New Testament, in I Peter 4:1: "Remembering that Christ endured bodily suffering, you must arm yourselves with a temper of mind like his."

⁷ Matt. 10:34; 11:12; Luke 16:16; 22:36 ff.

8 In addition to the passages already quoted the main texts of Paul and his disciples are I Cor. 9:7, 25; II Cor. 6:7; 10:3 ff.; I Thess. 5:8; Eph. 6:11 18; I Tim. 1:18; II Tim. 2:3-5.

9 Adolf Harnack pointed to this in his famous study *Die Mission und Ausbreitung des Christentums in den ersten drei Jahrhunderten* (Leipzig, 1903; English edition: New York, 1904), III, chap. iii. He then wrote a monograph on this subject: *Militia Christi: Die christliche Religion und der Soldatenstand in den ersten drei Jahrhunderten* (Tübingen, 1905). Many studies have been published since. Cf., e.g., Jean-Michel Hornus, *Evangile et Labarum* (Geneva, 1960) and the literature indicated there.

10 A. Harnack, *Militia Christi*, pp. 35, 40 f.

11 *Ibid.*, pp. 68 f.; 122; and J.-M. Hornus, *op. cit.*, p. 56. The linguistic development of the term *paganus* was very complex. In the Byzantine world, where the *militia Christi* terminology was less common, *paganus* was also interpreted as meaning "a villager" because paganism survived longer in the rural areas than in the cities.

12 J.-M. Hornus, *op. cit.*, p. 55, referring to C. Mohrmann, "Statio," in *Vigiliae Christianae*, VII (1953), 221-45.

13 A. Harnack, *op. cit.*, p. 19.

14 Neither Paul nor any other New Testament writer used such terms as *hierarchē* and *hypertagē* when referring to those who were given special tasks and offices in and for the church. Even the usual term for government (*archē*) is never used in the New Testament to designate church authorities. All authority (*exousia*) derives from the triune God and expresses itself in service (*diakonia*). In the church, authority always takes the form of *hypotagē* (submission): first of all submission to the authority of God and, consequently, mutual submission of the ministering church to its ministers and vice versa. The congregations have to submit themselves to the authority of the apostles and to those who labor among them insofar as Christ, the one essential Minister, serves through them (I Cor. 16:16; I Thess. 5:12; Heb. 13:17). Yet these ministers, even the apostles, had to submit themselves to the authority and discernment of the congregations (Acts 17:11); the congregation as a whole was therefore made responsible for the life of the church and the conduct of its ministers (I and II Cor. and Rev. 2-3).

15 A. Harnack, *op. cit.*, p. 16.

16 A remark of bishop Stephen C. Neill, quoted in the introduction to Robin McGlashan, "Conversion—A Comparative Study" in *Documents from the Department on the Laity*, VIII (Geneva, 1960). Cf. also Julius Schniewind, "The Biblical Doctrine of Conversion," in *Scottish Journal of Theology*, V (1952), 267-81 and Eric Routley, *The Gift of Conversion* (Philadelphia, 1955).

17 The most thorough study is still the one of Yves M.C. Congar, O.P., *Lay People in the Church: A study for a theology of Laity* (London, 1957). The most read and discussed Protestant book on the subject is probably the one of Hendrik Kraemer, *A Theology of the Laity*, (London, 1958). Some other recent publications are: Dorothee Hoch, *Gott liebt die Welt; Versuch einer neuen Schau von Kirche und Welt, Pfarrer und Laien* (Zurich, 1958); Arnold B. Come, *Agents of Reconciliation* (Philadelphia, 1960), Howard Grimes, *The Rebirth of the Laity* (New York/Nashville, 1962); Francis O. Ayres, *The Ministry of the Laity* (Philadelphia, 1962); and Kathleen Bliss, *We the People* (London, 1963). For a comprehensive Roman Catholic bibliography see *L'Apostolato Dei Laici* (Milan, 1957) and for a Protestant/Orthodox bibliography see *Laici in Ecclesia: An Ecumenical bibliography on the Role of the Laity in the Life and Mission of the Church* (Geneva, 1961).

18 This is true, for instance, for the term *ryomai* which means to defend, rescue, liberate and save somebody who is attacked and accused. The attacks do not come only from human enemies (Luke 1:71; Rom. 15:31; II Thess. 3:2; II Tim. 4:17 f.). Behind them stands the power of death (Rom. 7:24; II Cor. 1:10), the powers of darkness (Col. 1:13) and therefore the power of the evil one (Matt. 6:13) who accuses us at the last judgment (I Thess. 1:10). It is always God who rescues. Salvation is a gift, but a gift which comes out of God's combat with the powers and principalities. Cf. *T.W.z.N.T.*, VI, 999-1004 (W. Kasch) and the studies by G. Aulén and R. Leivestad mentioned earlier.

19 Eric Routley concluded his study on conversion with the following summary statements: "Primarily 'conversion' in Biblical thought means stopping, turning and attending. —Its consequence is an experience of freedom and light. —It is characteristic of the converted man that he welcomes the duty that Christ lays on him; his whole attitude to 'duty' is now different. —Conversion is wrought by God through the Holy Spirit. —Conversion takes its pattern from the Death and Resurrection of Jesus Christ. —Conversion is a free gift, neither the direct consequence of effort by the believer nor meritable to him. —But conversion requires a certain preparedness in the believer. —Conversion is primarily a matter of being, and only secondarily a matter of morals. —Conversion produces a real man, more himself than he could be in the unregenerate state. —Conversion acts upon anxiety and transforms it into Assurance; it acts upon fear and transforms it into courage; it acts on duty and transforms it into love" (*op. cit.*, p. 138).

20 In Matt. 28:19 baptism is in intimate relation with the act of becoming a disciple and the obedience to God's will. Acts 2:38; 9:18; Rom. 6:1 ff. show the connection between conversion and baptism, while the connection between faith and baptism is clearly stated in Acts 2:41; 8:12, 16:15-31 ff.; 18:8; Gal. 3:26 f.; Eph. 4:5; Col. 2:12.

21 For data see Joachim Jeremias, *Infant Baptism in the First Four Centuries* (London, 1960). The *oikos* formula (I Cor. 1:16; Acts 16:15; 16:30; 18:18) and the institution of proselyte baptism are, according to Jeremias, sufficient indirect evidence for the assumption that from New Testament times onwards children of parents joining the church were baptized together with their parents. With regard to the baptism of children of Christian parents Jeremias writes: "For the first century we have no special evidence for the baptism of Christian children. In the second it was already taken for granted" (p. 55).

22 This question is at present especially urgent in East Germany where the evil results of the century-long administration of cheap baptisms now become apparent. Because of this situation infant baptism becomes problematic, and there are instances of Lutheran pastors who no longer baptize their own children, not because they are in principle against infant baptism, but because they are convinced that the indiscriminate administration of infant baptism in the European majority churches no longer manifests God's costly grace but, rather, cheap grace. Cf. also the basic considerations by Rudolf Bohren, *Unsere Kasualpraxis: Eine missionarische Gelegenheit?* (Munich, 1960). Even in Great Britain an Anglican theological commission responsible for drafting a new baptismal liturgy suggested as the first and basic liturgy the one for believers' baptism, to which it added a liturgy for the baptism of children to be completed by a liturgy of confirmation (*Baptism and Confirmation: A Report submitted by the Church of England Liturgical Commission* [London, 1959]).

23 The Report of the Commission on Faith and Order on "The Meaning of Baptism" in *One Lord, One Baptism* (London, 1960), pp. 61 ff. states this clearly. It is interesting that the proposed union scheme for the church in

Ceylon and North India and Pakistan allows for practicing both infant and believers' baptism; see Stephen F. Bayne, *Ceylon, North India, Pakistan* (London, 1960), pp. 25 ff., 122 ff., 157 ff.

24 Important for regaining a biblical conception of church discipline is the text Matt. 18:15-20. The term *kerdainō* ("to win over") is the dominant note in this text, and all depends on the presence of the Lord who is present not only among his disciples but also among "pagans and tax-collectors." The disciplinary action is here not a self-complacent moral judgment, but the beginning of a "symphony" of intercession (vs. 19) so that those under discipline may be won back into full communion with the Lord. Biblical discipline has first of all a missionary and not a moralistic purpose. C. H. Dodd thinks that the verb *kerdainō* may have been a quasi-technical term in early Christianity in both Jewish-Christian and pagan-Christian congregations; cf.I Peter 3:1 and the practical working out of this "winning over" in I Cor. 9:19-22, 5:1-2 and the paraphrase in Gal. 4:1-2. Cf. C. H. Dodd, *New Testament Studies* (Manchester, 1953), pp. 58 ff.

25 Georg F. Vicedom, *Die Taufe unter den Heiden* (Munich, 1960), p. 49. In that church there is seldom a baptismal service without one or more dramatizations which manifest the connection between conversion and baptism. For examples see A. C. Frerichs, *Anutu Conquers in New Guinea* (Columbus, 1957), pp. 138 ff.

26 The corporateness of the militant church is especially underlined by the abundance of *syn*-compounds in the New Testament. Related to the *militia Christi* terminology are: *synagōnizomai*—strive together with (Rom. 15:30); *synathleō*—strive together for (Phil. 1:27; 4:3); *synaichmalōtos*—fellow prisoner (Rom. 16:7; Col. 4:10; Philemon 23); *synkakopatheō, synkakoucheō, sympatheō, sympaschō*—suffer affliction with (II Tim. 1:8; 2:3; Heb. 11:25; 10:34; Rom. 8:17; I Cor. 12:26; *systratiōtēs*—fellow soldier (Phil. 2:25; Philemon 2).

27 For texts from Church Fathers substantiating this ordination aspect of baptism see George Huntston Williams, "The Ancient Church," in Stephen C. Neill and Hans-Rudi Weber (ed.), *The Layman in Christian History* (London, 1963), pp. 30 ff. Cf. also Alan Richardson, *An Introduction to the Theology of the New Testament* (London, 1958), pp. 337-63; and Max Thurian, *Confirmation: Consécration des laïcs* (Neuchâtel/Paris, 1957).

28 L. Vischer, *op. cit.*, p. 42. The whole *Order of Service for the Reception of Baptized Persons into the Full Membership of the Church commonly called Confirmation* is published by the Oxford University Press (London, 1950).

29 L. Vischer, *op. cit.*, p. 38.

30 This theologically significant and generally accepted derivation is probably wrong etymologically. In the ancient church the term laity was most probably derived from the general use of the word *laikos*—belonging to the *plebs*, the common non-consecrated profane people. Cf. Ign. de la Potterie, "L'origine et le sens primitif du mot 'laïc' " in *Nouvelle Revue Théologique*, LXXX (1958), 840-53.

31 "Orthodox Views on the Ministry of the Laity," in *Documents from the Department on the Laity*, IV (Geneva, 1957).

32 The term "set apart" (*aphorizō*) is often used and equally often criticized in this connection. "To be set apart" translated into Aramaic means "a Pharisee." Thus, if one uses this term, the danger of pharisaism is always near, yet it is one of the several biblical terms used for designating the action by which God singles out something or somebody for a definite purpose. Together with *aphorizō* such terms as to call (*kaleō*), to choose (*eklegō*), to appoint (*tassō*), to entrust (*pisteuō*), to lay on hands (*cheirotoneō*) must be studied in

order to grasp the full meaning of the act of setting apart. *Aphorizō* occurs in the New Testament in connection with the following three acts: (1) In the last judgment the Son of man will set apart men into two groups: Matt. 25:31 ff.; 13:49. This setting apart happens neither at the basic ordination of baptism nor at any subsequent ordination. (2) The church is set apart from the world (Lev. 20:24), when the preaching of the gospel is rejected (Acts 19:9), when church members are persecuted (Luke 6:22) or when Christians become nonconformists because of the demands of the gospel (II Cor. 6:17, but see also the perversion of this in Gal. 2:12!). In missionary situations this second kind of setting-apart happens mostly in connection with baptism. (3) Within this "set apart people" certain persons are set apart for a special ministry or task (Rom. 1:1; Gal. 1:15; Acts 13:2). Especially this third kind of setting-apart is never mainly a setting-apart *from*, but always primarily a setting-apart *within* and *for*. It becomes then almost synonymous with "delegate" and "commission". —*T.W.z.N.T.*, V, 454 ff. (K. L. Schmidt).

CHAPTER 2

[1] Cf. J. T. Milik, *Ten Years of Discovery in the Wilderness of Judaea* (London, 1959).

[2] 1QM. English translation in Theodor H. Gaster, *The Dead Sea Scriptures* (New York, 1956), pp. 281-306. Cf. also J. T. Milik, *op. cit.* pp. 39 f., 94 ff., 121 ff. Leonhard Rost, "Zum Buch der Kriege der Söhne des Lichts gegen die Söhne der Finsternis" in *Theologische Literaturzeitung*, LXXX (1955), 205-8. *T.W.z.N.T.*, V, 297-300 (Kuhn). *T.W.z.N.T.*, VI, 511 f. (Bauernfeind).

[3] This is the hypothesis of Milik, which seems more convincing than the hypothesis of Rost, Bauernfeind and others according to whom the scroll is much older, dating from the second century B.C. Milik bases his theses on the extensive Hebrew commentary of 1QM by Y. Yadin (*The Scrolls of the War of the Sons of Light against the Sons of Darkness* [Jerusalem, 1955]), who compared it carefully with Roman treatises *De re militari*. Whatever hypothesis one follows, it is clear that the War Scroll gives a onesided picture of the community of Qumrân and that, e.g., the Manual of Discipline (1QS) reveals another (earlier or later?) phase of the community.

[4] Only after the completion of this manuscript was I kindly referred to the comparative study of Martin H. Scharlemann, *Qumran and Corinth* (New York, 1962). This study confirms much of the following comparison between the army of the War Scroll and the militant church, although Scharlemann compared the community of Qumrân as it is revealed to us through the *whole* Qumrân library with only one particular local church and although his *tertium comparationis* is different.

[5] Cf. G. von Rad, *Der heilige Krieg im alten Israel* (Zurich, 1951).

[6] Quoted from J.-M. Hornus, *op. cit.*, p. 61.

[7] Commenting on Hebrews 11:34 which refers to great leaders of Old Testament times who became "mighty in war," Bauernfeind writes: "This casualness [i.e., in speaking about the wars of the Old Testament] and the otherwise complete silence about these wars can only be understood in such a way that the thought about a restoration of holy wars, the justification for new holy wars to be carried out by the heirs of the New Covenant, is totally alien to the whole New Testament including the book of Revelation. . . ." "On the contrary, it is typical and by no means accidental that despite all the positive use of military images precisely the words *polemos* and *polemeō* or *machē* and *machomai*

never describe in a literal or figurative way what a Christian is supposed to do."
—*T.W.z.N.T.*, VI, 514 f.; cf. also IV, 533 f.

8 Cf. A. Harnack, *op. cit.*, pp. 46-92; J.-M. Hornus, *op. cit.*, pp. 73-154; C. J. Cadoux, *The Early Christian Attitude to War* (London, 1919).

9 The last great persecution of Christians under Diocletian and his colleagues began in the army and many Christian soldiers and officers died as martyrs. Their ultimate witness bore fruit: in 311 the emperor Galerius granted tolerance to the church and a year later Constantine gave his army the *labarum* (a banner with a cross) and under this sign his army was victorious against Maxentius, which meant that in 313 the church received full religious freedom. Only one year later, at the council of Arles in 314, the church revised its former theoretical pacifist attitude radically when in Canon III it ordered that "those who in times of peace throw their weapons away shall be excluded from the Eucharist." Desertion because of the Christian faith was not only disapproved of but punished with the severe penalty of excommunication. Military saints were proclaimed and the development leading up to the crusades began.

10 In this there is a marked difference between 1QM and I Maccabees 2:32 ff., according to which many Jews were killed because they would not fight on the Sabbath of the Lord.

11 Heinrich Schlier, "Zum Verständnis der Geschichte nach der Offenbarung Johannis," in *Die Zeit der Kirche* (Freiburg, 1958), pp. 265-74. *Nikaō, nikē*, etc., in *T.W.z.N.T.*, IV, 941-45 (Bauernfeind). R. Leivestad, *op. cit.*, pp. 212-38.

12 John Foster, *After the Apostles: Missionary Preaching in the First Three Centuries* (London, 1951) quotes a series of examples of this remarkable witness of early Christian women, pp. 39 ff. The exclamation of Libanius is quoted on p. 45.

13 Cf. L.-M. Dewailly, O.P., "Mission de l'Eglise et Apostolicité" and "Brève Histoire de l'Adjectif 'Apostolique'" in *Envoyé du Père; mission et apostolicité* (Paris, 1960), pp. 46-113 and 114-40. Cf. the Dutch literature on the theology of the apostolate, e.g., H. Berkhof, "De Apostoliciteit der Kerk," in *Nederlands Theologisch Tydschrift* (1947-48), pp. 146-60, 194-201; A. A. van Ruler, *Het apostolaat der kerk en het outwerpkerkorde* (Nijkerk, 1948); J. C. Hoekendijk, "Rondom het apostolaat," in *Wending* (1952), pp. 547-66; A. A. van Ruler, "Theologie des Apostolates," in *Evangelische Missionszeitschrift*, XI (1954), 1-21.

14 This has been convincingly shown in the scholarly study of Antony T. Hanson, *The Pioneer Ministry* (London, 1961).

15 *Report on Christ and the Church*, Faith and Order Paper No. 38 (Geneva, 1963), p. 54. The term "basic apostolic succession" is used in the contribution of the Department on the Laity to the Fourth World Conference on Faith and Order at Montreal, 1963: "Christ's Ministry through his whole Church and its Ministers," in *Laity*, No. 15 (Geneva, 1963), pp. 13-39.

16 For the following I am especially indebted to the Dutch literature on the theology of the apostolate, especially the study of H. Berkhof; cf. also my article on "The Laity in the Apostolic Church," in *The Ecumenical Review*, X/3 (1958), 286-93.

17 See H. Kraemer's statement that "communication of" is only possible within the context of "communication between" in *The Communication of the Christian Faith* (Philadelphia, 1956), chap. 1.

18 T. W. Manson, *Ministry and Priesthood: Christ's and Ours* (Richmond: John Knox Press, 1958), p. 21.

19 *Ibid.*, p. 21.

20 The Faith and Order report on *Christ and the Church* quoted earlier states on p. 57: "In their initial calling the Twelve were given a double function.

They are the nucleus of the reformed Israel, and at the same time they have a mission to Israel."

21 For examples of such spontaneous pioneer witness by laymen see the chapter on "The Younger Churches" in Stephen C. Neill and Hans-Rudi Weber (ed.), *op. cit.*, pp. 341 ff. Cf. also Paul Löffler, *The Layman Abroad in the Mission of the Church* (London, 1962).

CHAPTER 3

1 *The Deeds of the deified Augustus, who subjugated the whole World to the domination of the Roman People, and his liberalities to the state and people of the Romans.* This account was made by Augustus himself in his seventy-sixth year and, at his own request, was inscribed on two bronze columns at his tomb. These columns have been lost, but an almost contemporary copy was preserved. Full text in Ernst Hohl, "Die römische Kaiserzeit," in *Propyläen Weltgeschichte,* II (Berlin, 1931), inserted between pp. 368-69.

2 Andreas Alföldi, "Römische Kaiserzeit" *Historia Mundi,* IV (Bern, 1956), 255-60.

3 *T.W.z.N.T.,* V, 591 f., on *opsōnion* (Heidland).

4 *Charisma* was also used outside the Roman army with a more general meaning. In a papyrus found in Egypt somebody classified his possessions in two columns, one *apo agorasias* (what has been bought) and one *apo charismatos* (what has been freely received). In the New Testament the term occurs seventeen times, fourteen times in Pauline letters, twice in the Pastoral letters and once in I Peter. Especially in German there is a growing literature about the term and its significance for the church, its members and its ministers. Cf. Georg Eichholz, *Was heisst charismatische Gemeinde?* (Munich, 1960) and the literature indicated there. I have dealt with the substance of this chapter in the essay "The Laity: its Gifts and Ministry" which is published in the volume of essays in honor of W. A. Visser 't Hooft called *The Sufficiency of God,* edited by Robert C. Mackie and Charles C. West (London, 1963), pp. 187-206.

5 Rom. 12:6-8; I Cor. 12:8-10, 28-30. Perhaps also Eph. 4:11, although the technical term *charisma* is not used, but the more general term *dōrea* (in connection with *charis* in vs. 7) which in the New Testament always means a gift from God.

6 These verbs are used in connection with the *charismata* in Rom. 1:11; I Peter 4:10; Rom. 11:29; I Tim. 4:14; I Cor. 12:31; II Tim. 1:6.

7 Charismatic enthusiasm has never died out in church history. When the early church began to settle down in the structures of early Catholicism the rising monastic movement displayed charismatic enthusiasm. So did many of the sects and pre-Reformation movements during the Middle Ages and the Movements of the Radical Reformation since. Revivals are almost always accompanied by charismatic enthusiasm, and the contemporary Pentecostal Movement, which is by no means restricted to Pentecostal churches, reminds us forcefully that the Spirit can indeed manifest itself in enthusiasm.

8 In his study "Geist und Enthusiasmus: Eine Erläuterung zur Paulinischen Theologie" in *Studien zu Paulus* (Zurich, 1954), pp. 107-24, G. Schrenk showed that the terms *enthusiasmos* and *ekstasis* were technical terms in the mystery religions of the time of the early church. Their aim was to replace the human *nūs* (intelligence and moral judgment) with the Deity. According to Paul, however, the Spirit does not replace but, rather, renews and guides the *nūs* in

order to use it for God's purpose. Cf. also *T.W.z.N.T.*, VI, 330-453, on *pneuma* (Schweizer).

⁹ The term *charisma* plays an important role in Max Weber's writings. However, he equates the charismatic with the enthusiastic and is therefore led to speak about "charismatic domination" *(charismatische Herrschaft)* contrary to Paul who always wrote about charismatic *service*. Cf., e.g., *Wirtschaft und Gesellschaft* (Tübingen, 1956), pp. 140-48, 555-58, 662-95.

¹⁰ This is made clear in the study by Karl Rahner, S. J., "Das Charismatische in der Kirche," in *Das Dynamische in der Kirche* (Freiburg, 1958), pp. 68 f. According to Rahner each *charisma* has its *kairos*, its right time, and must therefore wait until that time has come. In this waiting a *suffering* is implied. Holy impatience must always be balanced with holy patience in the church.

¹¹ Cf. *panoplia* in *T.W.z.N.T.*, V, 295-97, 300-315 (Oepke); R. Leivestad, *op. cit.*, pp. 160 ff. and the earlier mentioned literature about powers and principalities.

¹² The long battle-sword *(romphaia)* with which Death appears in the book of Revelation (6:8) and which comes out of the mouth of Christ the judge (Rev. 1:16; 19:15) is never given to Christians and the church. The term used in Eph. 6:17 is *machaira* which originally meant the knife which was used, e.g., for preparing sacrifices. As a weapon *machaira* appears as dagger or short sword. —*T.W.z.N.T.*, IV, 530-33; VI, 993-98 (Michaelis).

¹³ In the Old Testament God appears several times as warrior in his full armor. Cf. Is. 42:13; 59:17; Ps. 35:1 ff. (Wisdom of Solomon 5:17-22). With this armor God fights against the enemies of his faithful (Ps. 7:11; 35:1 ff.; 91:4).

¹⁴ The verb *katargeō*, which is used in texts like I Cor. 2:6; 15:24, 26; II Thess. 2:8; II Tim. 1:10 and Heb. 2:14, is difficult to translate. The New English Bible uses the following twenty-one different English expressions to translate the twenty-six occurrences of *katargeō* in the New Testament: use up, cancel, undermine, go for nothing, for destruction, discharge, overthrow, passing, put an end, cease, vanish, finish, abolish, fade, abrogate, render ineffective, completely sever, to be no more, annul, destroy, break the power. There seems to be a tendency among Bible translators to choose the strongest words such as "abolish," "destroy," etc., when *katargeō* is used in connection with the powers and principalities and thus to suggest that the ultimate destiny of powers and principalities would be destruction. However, all these passages can also be translated with "overthrow" and "dethrone." On the basis of this H. Berkhof *(Christus en de Machten*, pp. 42 f.) suggests that, e.g., I Cor. 15:24, 26 does not speak about the annihilation of the powers and principalities and of death but about their dethronement. These powers are being disarmed by Christ as enemies and at the same time mobilized for God's service. Yet the New Testament does not really reveal to us what it means that even the powers and principalities are reconciled with God and share in the new life in Christ. Does death, for instance, have a place even in the new creation, not as a frightening enemy but as a servant of God? Can death now and in the kingdom of God be a *charisma*, namely the grace of "limited time"? Cf. for the question of *katargeō* and the powers and principalities also G. B. Caird, *op. cit.*, pp. 82 ff., and *T.W.z.N.T.*, I, 452-55 (Delling).

¹⁵ Where class structures, differences of race, nationality or educational background mark the church so strongly as to divide it, the church ceases to function as the training-ground for growth into maturity. Christians then choose their brothers and sisters in Christ and do not accept them as the *given* brothers and sisters. In modern industrial society where each man is at the center of a little world of relationships which he is increasingly free to organize as he

wishes and where, therefore, the *given* neighbor ceases to exist, the givenness of the brother in Christ becomes even more important. The full unity of Christians at the local level is thus a prerequisite if the church is to become militant. Cf. Lesslie Newbigin, "Four Talks on I Peter," in *We Were Brought Together*, Report of the National Conference of Australian Churches (Sydney, 1960), pp. 103 f., 107.

16 Dietrich von Oppen, "Frömmigkeit als Sachlichkeit," in *Universitas*, XVII (September, 1962), 999-1003.

17 This was clearly seen by the missionary scholar Roland Allan. Cf. especially his less known writings now reprinted in the volume *The Ministry of the Spirit*, ed. by David M. Paton (London, 1960). The essay on "Mission Activities Considered in Relation to the Manifestation of the Spirit" (pp. 87-113) refers particularly to this point.

CHAPTER 4

1 Illustration No. 29 in F. van de Meer and Christine Mohrmann, *Atlas of the Early Christian World*, has a map with the various ancient house-churches which could be located in Rome.

2 *Ibid.*, which shows a photograph of this Mithraeum (No. 33). For the following see M. J. Vermaseren, "Mithras," in *Religion in Geschichte und Gegenwart* (3. Aufl.), IV 1020-22; Rudolf Bultmann, *Das Urchristentum im Rahmen der antiken Religionen* (Zurich, 1949), pp. 169-75; A. Harnack, *op. cit.*, pp. 38 ff. and his appendix on "The spread of Christianity and the spread of Mithraism" in *The Expansion of Christianity*, II, 447-51.

3 Prudentius, *Peristephanon* x. 1011-50, translation in C. K. Barrett, *The New Testament Background: Selected Documents* (London, 1961), pp. 96 ff.; cf. also pp. 102-4.

4 Cf. *T.W.z.N.T.*, III, 180-90, on *thysia* (Behm), III, 249-52, 257-84, on *hiereus* (Schrenk), V, 492-95, on *osmē* (Delling), V, 835-40, on *paristēmi* (Bertram/Reicke); T. W. Manson, *op. cit.*, pp. 26-31, 35-72; Antoinette Butte, *Les offrandes sacrificielles du chrétien dans le Nouveau Testament,*" unpublished thesis (Theological Faculty, Montpellier, 1959).

5 T. W. Manson, *op. cit.*, p. 63.

6 Cf. Ernst Kinder, "Allgemeines Priestertum im Neuen Testament," in *Schriften des Theologischen Konvents Augsburgischen Bekenntnisses*, Heft 5 (Berlin, 1953); A. Richardson, *op. cit.*, pp. 295-303; T. W. Manson, *op. cit.*, pp. 35-72. The Reformers held varying conceptions: "It would thus seem that the Calvinist view leaves no place in the Church for priesthood. To call the Christian Community 'a royal priesthood' is no more than to confer on its members an honorary status without any defined function. For Zwingli the Christian as priest offers himself to God; for Luther his function is that of intercession for his fellow members. The main strains of Reformation theology are not at one regarding the priesthood of believers" (T. W. Manson, p. 37). Cf. also Hans Storck, *Das allgemeine Priestertum bei Luther* (Munich, 1953); T. F. Torrance, *Royal Priesthood* (London, 1955); Y. M. J. Congar, *op. cit.*, pp. 112-221, and William Robinson, *Completing the Reformation, the Doctrine of the Priesthood of all Believers* (Lexington, 1955). For a critique of this concept as the starting point for a theology of the laity see H. Kraemer, *A Theology of the Laity*, pp. 61 ff. and 93 ff.

7 T. W. Manson, *op. cit.*, pp. 64, 70.

8 Franz J. Leenhardt, *The Epistle to the Romans* (London, 1961), pp. 300 ff.;

H. Schlier, "Vom Wesen der apostolischen Ermahnung nach Römerbrief 12:1-2" in *Kirche in der Zeit*, pp. 74-89. Ernst Käsemann, "Gottesdienst im Alltag der Welt (zu Röm. 12)" in *Judentum, Christentum, Kirche, Festschrift für Joachim Jeremias* (Berlin, 1960), pp. 165-71; Pierre Bonnard, "The Discernment of God's Will in the Early Church," in *Laity*, No. 10 (Geneva, 1960), pp. 5-11.

9 The main texts are *Eph. 5:2* where it is said that Christ gave himself up on our behalf "as an offering [*prosphora*] and sacrifice [*thysia*] whose fragrance [*osmē*] is pleasing to God." This happened once for all at the cross, but it continues to happen in the life and suffering of all Christians and of the apostolic ministers. In *Rom. 12:1* the total Christian existence is called a sacrifice (*thysia*) which is offered (*paristēmi*) by the Christians themselves, while in *Col. 1:28* this Christian existence is offered (*paristēmi*) by the apostle. It is not quite clear who offers and what is offered in the passages Phil. 2:17 and Rom. 15:16 which are both very difficult to translate. Does, according to Phil. 2:17, Paul offer the faith of the Philippians, being in the process of this offering himself spent as a libation (*spendomai*)? Or do the *thysia* and *leiturgia* refer to the fact that in faith the Philippians offer themselves and that the apostolic outpouring of his whole life in the service of the gospel is the libation which accompanies the offering of the Philippians? Does, in Rom. 15:16, the apostle as the minister (*leiturgos*) of Jesus Christ in his priestly service (*hierurgeō*) of the gospel offer the Gentile converts to God who thus become a sacrifice (*prosphora*)? Or is the purpose of Paul's priestly service among the Gentiles that the offering made by Gentiles (of themselves, as in Rom. 12:1) be well made? However these two passages may be interpreted, it is clear that according to *II Cor. 2:14-16* the apostolic preaching and in fact the apostolic ministers themselves are called "the incense [*osmē*] offered by Christ to God." Also acts of mercy are called "a fragrant offering [*osmē*], an acceptable sacrifice [*thysia*]" in *Phil. 4:18* and in *Heb. 13:16*, because this belongs essentially to a sacrificial life. So does of course also the praise and acknowledgment of God's name which in *Heb. 13:14* is equated with the bringing of a sacrifice up to the altar (*anapherō thysian*). All this is implied in the work of the royal priesthood which has "to offer spiritual sacrifices" [*anapherō thysias*], according to *I Peter 2:5*.

10 It is misleading to translate *aiōn* in Rom. 12:2 with "world." Paul referred here to the present age that is ruled by "governing powers, which are declining to their end" (I Cor. 2:6, 8). This age is therefore an "age of wickedness" (Gal. 1:4) and those who live in it are always in danger that their minds will be "blinded by the god of this passing age" (II Cor. 4:4). This wicked spirit of the present age imposes on us criteria of judgment which do not really matter (I Tim. 6:17). The Christian answer to this danger is not an exodus out of this *aiōn* (I Cor. 5:10), but conversion, nonconformity and the continuous struggle of faith, because ultimately, in and behind this *aiōn*, Christians face the rebellious powers and principalities. In Eph. 2:2 the term is perhaps even used to designate a personification of cosmic powers, parallel to the reference, immediately following, to the "commander of the spiritual powers of the air" *T.W.z.N.T.*, I, 197-208 (Sasse).

11 R. Leivestad, *op. cit.*, pp. 178-92.

12 The military terminology is intimately connected with the athletic imagery, cf. *T.W.z.N.T.*, I, 134-40, on *agōn, agōnizomai, agōnia* (Stauffer) and I, 166 f., on *athleō, athlēsis* (Stauffer). Like the one who runs a race in the stadium the militant church has an *aim* towards which everything must be directed (Luke 13:24; I Thess. 2:2; Col. 1:29; II Tim. 4:7 f.; I Tim. 6:12). This race and struggle

106   THE MILITANT MINISTRY

implies *discipline and utter renunciation* (I Cor. 9:25, 27; II Tim. 2:5; 4:5; I Tim. 4:7 ff.). It is a *struggle against* opponents and therefore *dangerous* (Phil. 1:28; Heb. 12:3 f.; 11:33; I Thess. 2:2; II Cor. 7:5; Jude 3). Therefore this *agōn* and this *athlēsis* are most often connected with suffering and martyrdom (II Tim. 4:6; I Tim. 6:11 f.; Heb. 10-12 passim). This is not an egoistic struggle, but a *struggle for the many* (Col. 2:1 f.; 4:12 f.; Rom. 15:30). All these elements are brought together in Phil. 1:27 ff. The agony of Christ and the militant church is not a fear of suffering and death but the fear concerning the victory (Luke 22:44).

13 *Kopos and kopiaō* became technical terms for the work of the apostolic ministers. *Kopos* is the fatigue which comes from a continuous battle or any other exhausting work, but it means also the complete devotion to tiring work. In the New Testament this second meaning predominates (with the exception of John 4:6 and Rev. 2:3). Paul must have liked this term and he began to use it in a specific way for designating his own apostolic work and suffering (I Cor. 15:10; I Thess. 2:9; II Cor. 11:23; Col. 1:29 etc.), but also the work and suffering of other apostolic ministers (I Cor. 15:58; II Cor. 10:15; I Thess. 5:12 etc.). —*T.W.z.N.T.*, III, 827-29 (Hauck).

14 For this and the following see A. T. Hanson, *op. cit.*, passim, summarized in his *The Church of the Servant* (London, 1962), pp. 45-60.

15 The question of non-professional ministers is again becoming acute in all confessions and on all continents. Cf. Roland Allen, *The Case for Voluntary Clergy* (London, 1940), a summary of which is contained in *The Ministry of the Spirit*, pp. 135-89; Robin Denniston (ed.), *Part-Time Priests?* (London, 1960); *A Tent-Making Ministry*, (WCC, Geneva, 1962).

16 Cf. "A Mature Minority" in *Laity*, No. 8 (Geneva, 1959), pp. 28-41 and the literature on the diaspora situation on pp. 41 f.

17 *L'expérience humaine du Sacrifice* (Paris, 1948). The study consists of four large chapters dealing with "The forms of exchange as an antecedent to sacrifice" (pp. 1-41), "The religious sacrifice" (pp. 42-119), "The sacrifice as structure of the ethical experience" (pp. 120-207) and "The sacrifice as a limit-experience: Sacrifice and transcendence" (pp. 208-59). The following short excerpts can in no way do justice to Gusdorf's profound meditation.

18 E. V. Matthew, "The Laity: the Church in the World," in *Laity*, No. 13 (Geneva, 1962), pp. 11 f.

CHAPTER 5

1 René Voeltzel, *Le rire du Seigneur: Enquêtes et remarques sur la signification théologique et pratique de l'ironie biblique* (Strasbourg, 1955).

2 The story of the conversion of the jailer in Philippi probably contains some reminiscences of actual happenings. It is told in the style of legendary liberation stories which were quite popular during the first century and for which the author of the Acts must have had a special liking (cf. 5:19-27; 12:6-11).

3 Paul and his disciples used the image of the prisoner of war (*aichmalōtos*) for the struggle of faith. Man is a prisoner of sin (Rom. 7:23), but in the battle of faith Paul and his fellow soldiers demolish strongholds of pride and make every human thought a war prisoner of Christ (II Cor. 10:4-5). The apostolic ministers themselves become "captives in Christ's triumphal procession" (II Cor. 2:14) and Paul could therefore call his fellow workers *synaichmalōtoi* (Rom. 16:7; Col. 4:10; Philemon 23). Yet through Christ's victory not only the militant

church and its ministers are Christ's war prisoners, but all, including the powers and principalities (Eph. 4:8; Col. 2:15).—T.W.z.N.T., I, 195-97 (Kittel), and III, 159 f. (Delling).

⁴ Hans von Campenhausen, "Die Heiterkeit der Christen," in *Zeitwende* (Hamburg, 1956), pp. 235-46 (also in his *Tradition und Leben: Kräfte der Kirchengeschichte* [Tübingen, 1960], pp. 431-40); "Ein Witz des Apostel Paulus und die Anfänge des christlichen Humors," in *Neutestamentliche Studien für Rudolf Bultmann* (Berlin, 1957), pp. 189-193; "Christentum und Humor," in *Theologische Rundschau* (27/1, Tübingen, 1961), pp. 65-82. This last article consists mainly of a critical review of modern Christian writings about Christian humor. According to von Campenhausen the best publication on this subject is: Gerhard Jacobi, *Langweile, Musse und Humor und ihre pastoraltheologische Bedeutung* (Berlin, 1952).

⁵ Further information about the *risus paschalis* and the humor of the medieval church in Gerd Heinz-Mohr, *Sermon, ob der Christ etwas zu lachen habe* (Hamburg, 1959), pp. 5 ff.

⁶ Fritz Blanke, *Luthers Humor: Scherz und Schalk in Luthers Seelsorge* (Hamburg, 1954). Heinrich Vogel, "Der lachende Barth: Ein Essay über den Humor als Stilelement im theologischen Denken Karl Barths," in *Antwort, Festschrift für Karl Barth* (Zollikon, 1956), pp. 164-71.

⁷ The quite common term *eudaimonia* never occurs in the New Testament. *Hēdonē* is used five times and always in a pejorative way. *Hilaros* and *hilarotes* occur once each (II Cor. 9:7; Rom. 12:8). The term *eupsycheō* which is found quite frequently on tombs and sometimes in letters of consolation in the Hellenistic world occurs only once (Phil. 2:19). Even the words *Euphrainō* and *euphrosynē* which played a great role in the Greek translation of the Old Testament are seldom used in the New Testament and then mostly in Old Testament quotations or for everyday joys (Luke 12:19; 15:23 f., etc.; II Cor. 2:2). The joy of faith, however, is expressed with the terms *agalliaomai* (11 times), *agalliasis* (5 times), *chairō* (71 times) and *chara* (59 times) which comes significantly enough from the same root as *charis, charisma*. The joy of faith is an abundant and gracious joy.

⁸ For the following see the careful exegetical study of E. G. Gulin, *Die Freude im Neuen Testament* (Helsinki, I Teil, 1932; II Teil, 1936); J. J. von Allmen (ed.) *Vocabulary of the Bible* (London, 1958), article on "joy," pp. 207 f.; *T.W.z.N.T.*, I, 18-20, on *agalliasis*, (Bultmann), and II, 770-73, on *euphrosynē*, (Bultmann).

⁹ G. F. Vicedom, *op. cit.*, p. 27.

¹⁰ R. Voeltzel, *op. cit.*, pp. 157-62. E. G. Gulin, *op. cit.*, I, 153-62. See especially the hymns of victory in Rom. 8:31-39 and I Cor. 15:54-57.

¹¹ Those who have heard and understood the gospel can no longer boast in any personal or national religious privileges or achievements. Paul rejected radically all those who put their confidence in such external things (Phil. 3:3 ff.), yet he retained the term "to boast" *(kauchaomai)*, using it to express the paradox of a Christian life: Christian boasting consists in the fact that all the old self-centered and self-confident boasting has radically passed. Only Christ and his cross can now be an occasion for boasting (Rom. 5:11; I Cor. 1:25-31; II Cor. 10:17; Gal. 6:14). While a religious man boasts in his achievements, the Christian boasts in his sufferings and weaknesses (Rom. 5:3; II Cor. 11:30), because in these God's power and Christ's life become manifest (II Cor. 4:10 f.; 12:9). This is also the reason for the apostle's boasting in his apostolic work (II Cor. 1:12 ff.; 10:8 ff.; 11:16–12:13) which develops from a "foolish" boasting into a truly Christian one, not based on any comparison between his work and the work

of others but on Christ who works, suffers and is victorious through the apostle. In all these texts, "to boast" is almost synonymous with "to give thanks" and "to rejoice."—*T.W.z.N.T.*, III, 646-54 (Bultmann). Gulin, *op. cit.*, I, 167, 208 ff.

[12] *Ibid.*, I, 123 ff. Oscar Cullmann, *Early Christian Worship* (London, 1953), pp. 15 ff.

[13] Cf. Otto Michel, "Gottesherrschaft und Völkerwelt," in *Evangelische Missions Zeitschrift* (Stuttgart, 1941), pp. 225-67; Ernst Lohmeyer, "Mir ist gegeben alle Gewalt: Eine Exegese von Matth. 28, 16-20," in *In memoriam E. Lohmeyer* (1951), pp. 22-49. A summary of the modern exegesis of Matt. 28:18-20 in J. Blauw, *The Missionary Nature of the Church* (London, 1962), pp. 83-88.

[14] *Das Buch der Heiligen Gesänge der Ostkirche* (Hamburg, 1962), pp. 18 f., 25 f., 102-14, 165 f. The hymns are translated into English in *The Services for Holy Week and Easter Sunday* (Brookline, 1952). The following renderings of the hymns are free translations.

[15] Even during his earthly life Jesus went before (*proagō*) his disciples who followed him (Mark 10:32) just as the astrologers followed the star which went before them (Matt. 2:9). Yet this pioneering quality of Christ is even more true after the resurrection (Mark 14:28; 16:7). He is, according to Heb. 6:20, our "forerunner" (*prodromos*). Christian mission does therefore not mean to bring Christ into a new country, culture or time, but to catch up with him and to discern him where he is already present as the King incognito.

[16] In Pauline writings there is an intimate connection between "joy" and "hope." Christians rejoice in the salvation and splendor which will be theirs (Rom. 5:2; 8:18). Yet because of the pledge of the Spirit given to us now (II Cor. 1:22) also the hope and joy become present realities. The apostle could therefore confidently speak about the present joy given by the God of hope (Rom. 15:13), about the continuous Easter festival of the Christian life (I Cor. 5:7 f.) so that Christians can and must always be joyful, because the Lord is near (I Thess. 5:16; Phil. 4:4 ff.). The kingdom of God which is now present in Christ through the power of the Spirit, is "joy in the Holy Spirit" (Rom. 14:17) —E. G. Gulin, *op. cit.*, I, pp. 162-79.

[17] One of the most interesting chapters in E. G. Gulin's study is his discussion of the deep interrelationship between Christian joy and the Pauline emphasis on the church's sharing in Christ's death and resurrection (I, pp. 214-51), of which the following are only a few excerpts.

[18] Cf. E. G. Gulin, *op. cit.*, I, 252-76. *Lypē* in *T.W.z.N.T.*, IV, 314-25 (Bultmann).

[19] Quoted in M. Schoch, *Der Gottesglaube des modernen Menschen* (Zürich, 1956), pp. 79 f.

[20] Christoph Blumhardt, *Christus in der Welt; Briefe an Richard Wilhelm*, ed. by Arthur Rich (Zurich, 1958).

[21] "The Logic of the Christian Mission," in *The Pilgrim*, III, No. 1 (1959), pp. 73 f. Cf. also M. M. Thomas' lecture at New Delhi on "The Challenge to the Churches in the New Nations of Africa and Asia," published only in German in *Neu Delhi Dokumente* (Witten, 1962), pp. 437-54.

[22] Pierre Teilhard de Chardin, *The Phenomenon of Man* (London, 1959); John Wren-Lewis, "Where is science taking us?" in *The Student World* (1958), pp. 249-68; Dietrich von Oppen, *Das personale Zeitalter* (Stuttgart/Gelnhausen, 1960); Denis Mumby, *The Idea of a Secular Society* (London, 1963); articles on "Secularization" in *The Student World* (1963), pp. 1-96; articles on the *Bulletin of the Christian Peace Conference* (Prague, since 1962).

[23] "The Finality of Jesus Christ in the Age of Universal History," in *Bulletin of the Division of Studies, World Council of Churches*, (Geneva, 1962), pp. 1-42.

[24] Michel Quoist, *Prières* (Paris, 1954), pp. 29, 35.